Better ENGLISH

Punctuation · Spelling · Grammar

Robyn Gee and Carol Watson

Designed and illustrated by Kim Blundell

English Punctuation: Contents

With thanks to Diccon Swan, and to Diana Bentley of the Reading Centre, University of Reading.

What is punctuation?

Punctuation is a collection of marks and signs which break words up into groups and give other helpful clues and information about their meaning. The purpose of punctuation marks is to make it easier for people to understand the exact meaning of written words.

This book explains the different uses of each punctuation mark and gives lots of tips and hints on how and where to use them. Here, you can see the complete range of punctuation marks to choose from.

.?!.,;:-() "" '' "" _ '

It might help you to understand exactly what punctuation marks do if you think about the difference between spoken words and written words.

When someone speaks they can do all sorts of things to help make the meaning of their words clearer to the person or people listening to them. They can vary their voice by making it higher or lower, or louder or softer; they can change the tone (or quality) of their voice and the speed at which they speak; and they can put in pauses of various different lengths. If the person listening can see, as well as hear, the person speaking, the expression on the speaker's face and the gestures they use, it can also help to communicate the exact meaning of their words.

Most people, without even thinking about it, use all these techniques to help them express the meaning of their words. In other words, these things act as "voice punctuation". When people don't use voice punctuation they are boring to listen to and difficult to understand. When children first learn to read aloud they usually ignore voice punctuation and this makes it hard to follow the meaning of the words they are reading.

Written punctuation cannot convey as much as voice punctuation, but it is still very important. It tells you how to turn the words into the right voice patterns to help you understand them. Today, once people have learnt to read, they usually do this inside their heads, but back in the Middle Ages anyone who could read and understand something without reading it aloud, or at least mouthing it, was considered very rare and talented.

Helping you read

One important thing that punctuation tells you is when and how long to pause when you are reading. The number and length of the pauses can make a great difference to the meaning of the words. You can see this by comparing the meaning of the two sentences below.

> **Charles I walked and talked half an hour after his head was cut off.**

> **Charles I walked and talked. Half an hour after, his head was cut off.**

At one time people used to write without putting any gaps between words. They then began to realize how helpful it would be to separate groups of letters into words, so that they could be converted back into speech more easily. The next step after separating the words was to put in punctuation marks for the pauses.

> **Atonetimepeoplewrotewithout puttinganygapsbetweenwords**

If you listen to people talking you will probably notice that their voices rise at the end of a question, but fall at the end of most other sentences. You can test this by getting someone to read the sentences below.

> **This is the best you can do.**

> **This is the best you can do!**

> **This is the best you can do?**

The rise and fall of a voice is called its intonation pattern and is often an important part of the meaning of spoken words. (In some languages, such as Chinese, the same word said with different intonations can mean totally different things.) Punctuation marks, especially question and exclamation marks, indicate what intonation you should use.

Are there any rules?

There are very few unbreakable rules of punctuation. Once you have learnt the basic uses of each mark, the way you punctuate can often be a matter of what you happen to prefer. Remember that there is often more than one perfectly correct way of punctuating a sentence. Concentrate on the clearest, simplest way of expressing something. The main thing to remember is

Is it useful?

that each mark should be useful. If a punctuation mark is not doing anything useful, leave it out.

When you are having difficulty trying to decide which punctuation marks to use in something you have written, it can be very helpful to say the words aloud and think about the pauses you use when you say them. A tape recorder can be even more helpful. It is very good practice to record yourself, or someone else, describing a scene or incident. Then play back the

recording, writing out your own words and putting in punctuation wherever you paused. Play back the recording again and check your written version against it.

In this book the main guidelines on how to use punctuation are given in the text. Examples which help to illustrate these guidelines are surrounded by blue borders.

> **She had a blue- eyed, big-eared, bird-brained boyfriend.**

A team of little punctuation experts make comments and suggestions to help pick out particular points.

Remember the capital letters

Test yourself

There are short tests on each section. These appear in yellow boxes so that you can spot them easily. There are also two pages of tests and quizzes on pages 26 and 27. The answers to all the tests are on pages 28 to 31. Always do the tests on a separate piece of paper.

In some sections you will find "Do" and "Don't" boxes. The "Don't" boxes warn of common mistakes and pitfalls to avoid. The "Do" boxes summarize the main points to remember about the more complicated punctuation marks.

Punctuation is very closely linked to grammar (the rules about the way words are used in a language), so you may come across the occasional grammatical term (e.g. "noun", "clause"). If you do not understand any of these terms or feel a bit hazy about the meaning, turn to the glossary on page 32 to check the exact meaning.

The rules and guidelines given in this book apply to English written by hand or on a typewriter. The printed English used in books, newspapers and magazines sometimes follows slightly different rules and conventions, so don't be put off if you see things in print which you would express differently in writing.

Full stops

Full stops (also called full points) do several jobs. They are the strongest punctuation mark, making the most definite pause.

1

They are used at the end of all sentences which are not questions or exclamations. (A sentence is a word, or group of words, which makes complete sense on its own.)

2

The witch stirred the cauldron.

This is a sentence

Stop.

Hello.

These are one word sentences.

Sentences usually have a noun and a verb, but they can, sometimes, consist of only one word.

3

Who are you?

Help!

A sentence can also be ended by a question mark, ? (see page 6) or an exclamation mark, ! (see page 7). In these cases you don't need a full stop.

4

The boy sat up. He got out of bed.

Don't forget the capital letter.

When you have used a full stop to end a sentence, remember to start the next sentence with a capital letter.

Stop the everlasting sentence

Remember the capital letters.

This is a very long sentence which does not make any sense. Can you put it right? There should be five full stops.

He trudged wearily along the dusty road his feet hurt and his head throbbed there was not a soul in sight for miles and he wondered what to do next then he saw someone waving at him at the top of the hill it was a tall man in a large hat

Three full stops in a row

You can use three full stops where part of a quotation or text is left out.

"Jack and Jill went up the hill . . . and Jill came tumbling after."

You can also use three full stops to show where a sentence is unfinished.

"He hid behind the gravestone and . . ."

I wonder what happened?

Notices, lists and labels

You don't use full stops in these.

No full stops here.

NO ENTRY

EXIT

PEKING
PARIS
ATHENS
TOKYO
ROME
MOSCOW

Shortening words by using full stops

Instead of writing some words in full you can cut them short, or "abbreviate" them, by just writing some of the letters, or just the first (initial) letters.

A full stop is used to show where letters have been left out, words shortened, or after initials.

Feb. 14th
Sun. 30th

Prof. (Professor)
Rev. (Reverend)

You can use a full stop to shorten the names of the days of the week and the months of the year. It is also used to shorten titles.

Dr – Doctor
Mr – Mister

No full stop here.

km – kilometre
mm – millimetre
cm – centimetre

Where the first and last letters in the shortened form are the same as in the full word, you can leave off the full stops if you want to.

Don't use full stops with abbreviations of metric measurements.

Joanna Jane Johnson
J. J. Johnson

Sometimes the first (initial) letter of a word is used to stand for the whole word. People's first names are often written as initials.

If an abbreviation comes at the end of a sentence, you don't need to use two full stops.

UN	**(United Nations)**
NATO	**(North Atlantic Treaty Organization)**
BBC	**(British Broadcasting Corporation)**
USA	**(United States of America)**

No full stop here.

You can leave out the full stops after initial letters of well-known organizations and place names.

▶ **They took the dog to the R.S.P.C.A.**

Short or long?

These words can be written in a much shorter way. How can you abbreviate them?

Victoria Cross
et cetera
Reverend John Williams
Professor Alexander Johnson
Saint Augustine
centimetre

Do you know what these abbreviations stand for?

A.A.	R.A.C.	Y.W.C.A.	R.S.P.C.A.

W.R.V.S.	St. John Ch. 4 v. 3	B.Sc.

You may need a dictionary.

Question marks

A question mark is used at the end of a sentence which asks a question. It is used instead of a full stop so the next word begins with a capital letter.

When the word or words in the sentence actually form a question it is called a *direct question*. This kind of sentence expects an answer.

Which is the best route to London?

An *indirect question* is a sentence which does not ask a question but tells you what question was asked. It does not have a question mark.

No question mark here.

He asked which was the best route to London.

A question can be just one word.

These are questions

Why? **Who?** **How?**

When? **What?**

Take care! If a sentence begins with one of these words it does not necessarily mean it is a question.

but this isn't.

When it is cold I wear my hat.

Uncertainty

Sometimes a question mark is used to show doubt about something like a date of birth. These should not be used in normal writing.

Question tags

A question can be tagged on to the end of a sentence.

It's not far, is it? I can get there tonight, can't I?

Question quiz

Which of these sentences do you think are questions?

1. Where is the hotel
2. He asked how much it would cost
3. Is it expensive
4. Will I like the food
5. What an awful room
6. It's a large room, isn't it
7. How long shall I stay

Exclamation marks

An exclamation mark is used at the end of a sentence or phrase to emphasize some special meaning within it.

It can mark surprise, humour or joy.

I don't believe it!

Silly me!

What a beautiful day!

It can show fear, anger, pain and danger.

Don't shoot!

How dare you!

Ouch!

When someone is giving an order or shouting, an exclamation mark is used.

Stand up straight!   **Halt!**

Attention!   **Call the police!**

An exclamation mark can sometimes appear in the middle of a sentence.

Good gracious! what has happened? ✓

Don't use one to make your own comment on something.

The fat lady ate fifty(!) cream buns. ✗

Don't

1. Don't use more than one exclamation mark at a time.

Wow!!!   **What!!**

2. Don't use them too often or they will lose their effect and make what you write boring to read.

> Too many here.

> Dear Polly
> How are you? I'm fine!
> I went to Jill's party
> last night! It was
> fantastic!! Didn't get
> home until 4am!!!
> Mum was furious — I
> can't go out for the
> rest of the week!
> Can you imagine!!!
> Oh well! See you.
> love Sue.

Commas

We ate chocolate, jelly and cake.

This makes it sound as though the jelly was made of chocolate.

We ate chocolate jelly and cake.

A comma is used to mark a brief pause, much shorter than a pause made by a full stop. It can be used to separate two words, or groups of words, in a sentence, in order to make the meaning clear.

Commas are the most common punctuation mark, but you have to be careful how you use them. You can easily change the meaning of a sentence by moving a comma to a different place or taking it away altogether.

Lists

When there is a list of words in a sentence, each word in the list is separated from the next by a comma.

They may be nouns,

or adjectives,

or verbs.

We will need hammers, nails and a saw.

Mr Cherry was a warm, hospitable man.

She stopped, stared and ran.

The last word in the list is usually joined to the the list by "and", instead of a comma.

The list may consist of groups of words divided by commas, instead of single words.

Sam frightens the cat, teases the dog, bullies his brother and annoys the neighbours.

There is no comma before the first word in the list, or after the last.

Try these

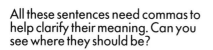

Can you see where the commas should be?

All these sentences need commas to help clarify their meaning. Can you see where they should be?

1. The monster was huge fat and spiky.
2. Everyone threw spears stones swords and boiling oil at the creature.
3. It roared growled spat and groaned but still it did not die.
4. A knight appeared wearing bright shining armour and pierced the beast with his special magic sword.
5. The huge beast screamed fell to the ground rolled over and died.
6. The king rewarded the knight with gold silver diamonds rubies and other precious things.

Long sentences

1

The comma comes before the joining word.

We queued for the concert for four hours, but we didn't manage to get tickets.

These two parts of the sentence are equally important.

Two or more simple sentences joined together by words like "but", "or", "nor", "so", "either" and "neither" are separated by a comma before the joining word.

2

When he saw the pirate ship on the horizon, the captain gave the alarm.

A sentence is sometimes made up of one main part (a main clause) with other, less important parts (subordinate clauses) joined to it by words like "when" "because" and "although". A subordinate clause is often separated from a main clause by a comma, especially if it comes before the main clause.

Sentence linking words

The joining words in long sentences are called conjunctions. Here are some more common conjunctions:

Beware! Some of these words are not always conjunctions.

after	if
before	unless
until	though
while	as
since	for

When you see any of these words think about using commas to separate the group of words they introduce from the rest of the sentence.

Commas with "and"

Commas are not generally used with "and". In a list "and" tends to replace the comma, but sometimes you need to use a comma before "and" to make the meaning absolutely clear.

The best horses in the race were Pacemaker, Starlight, Mr Speedy, Windstorm, and Thunder and Lightning.

Without this comma you might think there were four horses, or that the fourth horse was called Windstorm and Thunder.

Test yourself

Use the information above to help you.

Can you improve these sentences by adding commas?

1. The robber climbed through the window crept up the stairs and peered into the bedroom.
2. She called as loudly as she could but no-one could hear her.
3. The telephone was not far away yet there was little she could do to reach it.
4. She switched on all the lights so the man ran away in a panic.
5. The policeman who arrived later told her to put a lock on her window.

9

Inessential words and phrases

Commas are used to separate words or phrases in a sentence. The words enclosed by the commas could be left out without changing the general sense of a sentence.

Try reading these sentences through, then read them again, leaving out the words surrounded by commas.

Words like this are called sentence modifiers.

I felt, moreover, that he was being totally unreasonable.

Used for emphasis.

The book was, without doubt, the best she had read.

Describes Harry.

Harry Mann, our star player, broke his leg in the match last Saturday.

The man, who was wearing a blue hat, slid silently into the room.

But note this:

Men <u>who have beards</u> often smoke pipes.

These words are vital to the meaning of the sentence, so no commas are used.

Compare the two sentences below.

The trumpeters, who were playing in the overture, started to tune up.

In this sentence all the trumpeters present were part of the overture.

The trumpeters who were playing in the overture started to tune up.

This sentence suggests that there were trumpeters around who weren't taking part in the overture.

The commas change the meaning of these two sentences. They show that the words they surround are not essential to the meaning of the sentence.

Puzzle it out

Are the words in italics essential to the meaning of the sentence, or inessential?

1. The singer, *who was French,* had a very beautiful voice.

2. I felt, *however,* that he was unsuitable for the part.

3. The man *who was taller* would have been better.

4. He was, *without a doubt,* just as talented.

5. All the actors *in the opera* were of a very high standard.

Addresses and letters

You can use commas as above when writing addresses* and opening and closing letters.

> **The flight from Perth, Australia to London, England took 36 hours.**

Break up names of places with commas.

Dates and numbers

> **1,999,999**

Commas are used to break up groups of numbers into thousands.

> **February 14, 1990**   **February, 1990**

> **Spring, 1990**   Here the comma can be left out.

Commas are used in dates to separate the year, the day, month or season.

Comma moving puzzle

 Can you change the meaning of these sentences by moving or removing the commas?

1. The old lady collected all sorts of things: silver, paper, hats, clocks and tablecloths.

2. He had large, bright, green eyes.

3. She liked Rod, who played the drums, better than Jim.

Spot the mistakes

Some of the commas below are not necessary. Can you spot which ones?

The player, kicked the ball into the goal which was close by. The goalkeeper ran, jumped up, but missed it and the ball shot in. The spectators, who were delighted, shouted and screamed for joy. The referee, blew his whistle and waved his arms, around but the match continued.

Do

Do use commas:

1. To show a pause inside a sentence.
2. To separate the items on a list.
3. To separate inessential words or phrases from the rest of the sentence.
4. To break up numbers into thousands.
5. When writing a date.
6. When opening and closing letters. (For use of commas in direct speech see page 13.)

Remember that a comma should always help to make the meaning of a sentence clearer.

Don't

1. Use too many commas. If a sentence is broken by commas in too many places it makes it harder, instead of easier, to understand.

> **Flora came in, shouting out the news, that she had won, the competition.**

2. Break up a list of adjectives by commas, if they sound better without pauses.

> **They talked for hours about the good old days.**

When it does not make sense to put "and" in, don't put a comma in.

*See page 25.

11

Inverted commas

Inverted commas are also called quotation marks, quotes or speech marks. They are used in writing to show the exact words that someone has spoken. This is called direct speech.

Spoken words.

Inverted commas always appear in pairs.

Spoken words can be set out in three basic ways:

they can come at the beginning of a sentence,

> **"I have won a holiday for two in France," said Fred.**

they can come at the end of a sentence,

> **Fred said, "I have won a holiday for two in France."**

Use inverted commas only around the words actually spoken.

or they can come at the beginning and end of a sentence with an interruption in the middle.

> **"I have won," said Fred, "a holiday for two in France."**

Make the inverted commas curved and facing inwards.

Capital letters

A capital letter must be used whenever someone starts to speak,

Capital letter.

> **Alice asked, "How did you manage to win a holiday?"**

but do not use a capital letter unless it either starts someone's spoken words or starts a sentence.

No capital letter.

> **"How," asked Alice, "did you manage to win a holiday?"**

Reported speech

There are two ways of writing down what someone says. You can write down the person's exact words (direct speech) and put them in inverted commas, or you can report what they said in your own words. The second way is called reported or indirect speech. With reported speech you do not use inverted commas.

> **"I have always wanted to go to France," said Alice.**

> **Alice said that she had always wanted to go to France.**

Commas with inverted commas

In direct speech there must always be a comma between the introduction to speech (subject and "verb of saying") and the speech itself.

The verb of saying is often "says" or "said", but all these can be verbs of saying:

mutter	ask	declare
whisper	reply	comment
cry	exclaim	observe
shout	repeat	command

When the words spoken come before the verb of saying, they are followed by a comma,

> **"I am very excited about going abroad," said Fred.**

The comma goes inside the inverted commas.

but if the words spoken are a question or exclamation, use a question mark or an exclamation mark, not a comma.

> **"When are you going?" asked Alice.**

> **"You lucky thing!" she said.**

When the verb of saying and its subject start the sentence, they are followed by a comma.

> **Fred replied, "We are leaving tomorrow morning."**

The comma goes before the inverted commas.

The first word spoken has a capital letter.

When the spoken sentence is interrupted to insert a verb of saying and its subject, one comma is needed before breaking off the spoken words and another before continuing.

This comma goes inside the inverted commas.

This comma goes in front of the second pair of inverted commas.

> **"I do hope," said Alice politely, "that you and your friend have a wonderful time."**

This word is continuing the spoken sentence so it starts with a small letter.

Remember, also, to use commas:

round people's names, when they are spoken to by name, ▶

> **"I was wondering, Alice, if you would like to come with me," said Fred.**

round words like "yes", "no", "please" and "thank you", ▶

> **"Yes, of course I would."**

before question tags. ▶

> **"But I can't be ready to leave tomorrow morning, can I?"**

13

Punctuation patterns to remember

If you find it difficult to decide what punctuation marks to use with inverted commas and what order to put them in, the punctuation patterns below may help you. Look at all the different patterns and decide which one best suits the sentence you want to write. The red block represents the spoken words; the blue block represents the verbs of saying.

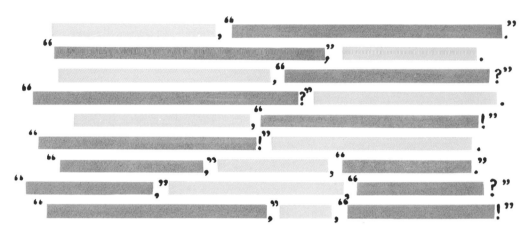

Commas, full stops, question marks and exclamation marks after spoken words usually come inside the closing inverted commas.

Turn nonsense into a conversation

(When you use inverted commas for a conversation always start a new paragraph when one person stops speaking and another starts.*)

Good morning, how are you today? the doctor asked. I feel dreadful, he replied gruffly. You should try to get up and walk about, she suggested. Then you might feel better. You must be joking! he exclaimed. Do you want a patient or a corpse?

Quotations

Pages 12 and 13 explain how inverted commas are used when you are quoting (repeating the exact words) that someone has said. They are also used when you quote the exact words from a book, newspaper or magazine.

Use full stops to show where you have left out some of the original words.

"One day. . . I was exceedingly surprised with the print of a man's naked foot on the shore, which was very plain to be seen in the sand." This was when Robinson Crusoe first realized there was another human on his island.

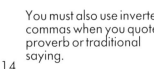

You must also use inverted commas when you quote a proverb or traditional saying.

Some people feel that "many hands make light work", but in my experience "too many cooks spoil the broth".

14

*See page 24.

Single inverted commas

> 'I have nothing to declare except my genius,' he said.

You can use single inverted commas instead of double ones, but single ones look rather like apostrophes,* which can cause confusion.

> "Who said 'I have nothing to declare except my genius' and when did he say it?" asked the quizmaster.

Sometimes you may need to use two sets of inverted commas in one sentence. This happens when you write a title or quote someone's words in the middle of a sentence that is already a quotation. The clearest thing to do is to use double inverted commas for the outer marks and single inverted commas for the inner marks.

Titles

> Use capital letters for the first word and any other important words.

> In printed material titles are often put in italics.

> Have you read "The Life and Adventures of Freddy the Frog"?

> Do not use capital letters for words like "a", "the", "and", "of", "at", "to", "in", "from", "on", "for".

You also need to use inverted commas when you write the titles of books, plays, films, newspapers, magazines, poems, songs, paintings and T.V. programmes.

Unusual words

Unusual words such as specialist terms, foreign words, slang and words used only in certain areas are often put in inverted commas. This helps to show the reader that they are unusual (and that the reader is not necessarily expected to know it already).

> He "flipped his lid".

> We stayed in a small "pension".

> The wind is "veering" when it changes in a clockwise direction.

Being funny

> Our "luxury" hotel turned out to be a concrete shed surrounded by a field of mud.

Inverted commas can help you to add an ironical, sarcastic or funny twist to something you write. You can put them round some words to give the word emphasis and show that you do not take it seriously.

Words quoted for discussion

> I have looked up "amnesia" in the dictionary hundreds of times, but I always forget what it means.

When you write a word, not simply for its meaning within a sentence, but in order to say something particular about it, you should put it in inverted commas.

Spot the title

Where should the inverted commas go?

1. He went to see Superman and E.T. last week.
2. They had good reviews in The Times.
3. I wanted to watch Coronation Street and Dallas so I didn't go with him.

*For apostrophes, see page 23.

15

Colons and semi-colons

Colons and semi-colons, like commas and full stops, mark the places where you would break or pause when speaking. You can get away without using them, but they can come in useful and it is worth knowing where you can use them.

Imagine that each punctuation mark has a certain strength according to how long a pause it represents. The comma is the weakest mark; then comes the semi-colon. The colon is stronger than the semi-colon, but weaker than the full stop.

Old-fashioned teachers used to tell their pupils to pause and count one at a comma, two at a semi-colon, three at a colon and four at a full stop. It might sound rather odd if you tried doing this, but it may help you to understand how to use colons and semi-colons.

How colons are used

1 A colon nearly always "introduces" or leads into something that is to follow. You may see it used before someone speaks or before a quotation.

> Don't forget that you have to use inverted commas* as well as colons here.

> He said:"I'll eat my hat."

> Remember the saying:"A stitch in time saves nine."

2 A colon is used to break a sentence when the second half of the sentence explains, expands or summarizes what comes in the first half.

> **Eventually he told us his secret: the old beggar was, in fact, a very rich man.**

> A colon used like this often means the same as "that is to say".

3 Colons are also used to introduce lists. Some people use a dash after the colon at the beginning of a list, but it is better to leave the dash out.

> **To make this pudding you will need the following ingredients: three ripe bananas, a pint of fresh cream, a small glass of brandy and some cherries and almonds for decoration.**

> Watch out for these phrases. All of them are quite often followed by a colon.

> **for example
> in other words
> to sum up
> the following
> as follows**

16

*For inverted commas see pages 12-13.

How semi-colons are used

1 A semi-colon can sometimes be used to replace a full stop. It links two complete sentences and turns them into one sentence. The two sentences should be closely linked in meaning and of equal importance.

The door swung open; a masked figure strode in.

> Here, a full stop would be a bit abrupt.

2 Semi-colons are often used before words like "therefore", "nevertheless", "however", "moreover", "consequently", "otherwise" and "besides", when these words link two independent clauses.

He never took any exercise; consequently he became very fat.

> Don't use semi-colons before ordinary conjunctions, like "and", "but", "for", "nor" and "or".

3 Semi-colons can also be used to break up lists, especially where each item on the list is rather long and using commas would be confusing.

> Sometimes you need to use commas as well as semi-colons to make the meaning of the sentence clearer.

> You *can* use a semi-colon before the word "and" when "and" introduces the last part of the list.

At the circus we saw a dwarf, juggling with swords and daggers; a clown who stood on his head on a tight-rope; a fire-eater with flashing eyes; and an eight-year-old lion tamer.

Deciding which one to use

If the first part of the sentence leads you forward to the information in the second part of the sentence, use a colon.

If the two parts of the sentence seem to be equally balanced, use a semi-colon.

There are times when it is difficult to decide whether to use a colon or a semi-colon.

The boy was like his father: short, fat and with a large nose.

Florence was very keen on swimming; her sister preferred cycling.

Do	Use a colon: 1. Before a list. 2. To introduce an explanation, expansion or summary of the first part of the sentence.	Use a semi-colon: 1. To join two closely linked sentences. 2. To break up lists.

Don't	Use a capital letter after either a colon or a semi-colon.

Brackets and dashes

Brackets are used in pairs around a group of words to keep them separate from the rest of the sentence. The words inside the brackets can also be referred to as "in parenthesis".

Brackets always appear in pairs.

I spoke to Eliza (her sister is a doctor) about your strange symptoms.

The streets were deserted (it was Easter Sunday) and not a single shop was open.

I gave the bear a banana (all I had left).

Interruption.

Explanation.

Afterthought.

If you take away the words between the brackets, the rest of the sentence should still make complete sense.

The words marked off by brackets introduce an extra idea into the sentence. This extra idea could be an explanation of something else in the sentence, an afterthought, or an interruption of the main idea in the sentence.

Full stops and commas with brackets

When you use brackets it is sometimes difficult to decide exactly where to put commas, full stops and other punctuation marks. First work out how you would punctuate the sentence if the words in brackets were not there.

(you all know what we have to do)

The rescue is tomorrow, but the plans may be changed any time.

A comma would normally come after the second bracket not before the first one.

We will need to take plenty of provisions (blankets, clothes, food and weapons).

If the words in brackets come at the end of a sentence, a full stop comes after the second bracket.

Wake me early. (Set your alarms for five o'clock.) We must leave before it gets light.

If the words in the brackets make a complete sentence and come between complete sentences, put a full stop inside the second bracket.

Double dashes

Dashes can be used in pairs, like brackets, to separate a group of words from the rest of a sentence. They are only used if the words they separate come in the middle of a sentence.

You could use brackets here.

Hannah invited her friends – there were ten boys and ten girls – to a fancy dress party.

Test yourself on brackets

These sentences need brackets to make sense. Can you think where they should go?

1. She got up early to go shopping the sales were on.
2. She went with Anne her best friend and the lady next door.
3. It took ages to travel home there was a bus strike and they returned exhausted.

Single dashes

Dashes, unlike brackets, do not always have to be used in pairs. For certain purposes they can be used singly. In some situations they are an alternative to brackets but they can also be used to mark an expectant pause.

1 **They tell me he is very kind – I don't know him.**

You could use brackets here.

A dash is often used to mark a pause or break before a sudden change of direction in a sentence. It may come before an afterthought added on to the end of a sentence.

List.

2 **Apples, pears, plums – all these grow in our orchard.**

You could use brackets here.

Summary. Summary.

List.

My favourite kind of fruit is citrus fruit – oranges, grapefruits, lemons, limes.

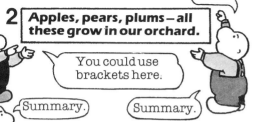

Sometimes a dash is used to separate a list from its summary. The summary may come before or after the list.

Pause for dramatic effect.

3 **I opened the lid eagerly and there inside the box was – a dead mouse.**

The part of the sentence after the dash is often surprising or unexpected. The dash gives you a moment of suspense before the surprise.

You could use brackets here.

4 **The jumper she made was full of mistakes – mistakes which you could sèe at a glance.**

Sometimes you may want to emphasize a particular word in a sentence by repeating it. If you do this, use a dash to separate the two identical words.

*For commas see pages 8-9.

Choosing between brackets and dashes

When you want to put words in parenthesis you have to choose whether to use brackets or dashes. This often depends on which you happen to prefer. If you can't decide, think about how strong a division you want to make between the words in parenthesis and the rest of the sentence.

Brackets mark the strongest division.

Dashes mark a less strong division.

If the words you want to separate are fairly close to the main meaning of the sentence, a pair of commas* may do the job quite well.

If you are still in doubt, it is probably safest to use brackets.

Practise your dashes

Where should the dashes go?

1. She decided to emigrate to Canada I don't know why.
2. She packed everything she could think of clothes, jewellery, books and records.
3. They drove on and on up the hill until at last, there to her delight was a beautiful old house.

Don't

1. Use double dashes if the parenthesis comes at the end of a sentence. Do use brackets or a single dash.
2. Use more than one pair of dashes in the same sentence.
3. Use double dashes and a single dash in the same sentence.
4. Put brackets within brackets.

Do

1. Use brackets or dashes to separate an interruption, explanation or afterthought from the main sentence.

19

Hyphens

The hyphen is half the length of a dash. It is a linking mark which joins two or more words together to make one word or expression.

Compound words

1 When two or more words are joined together they are called compound words. They can be compound nouns or compound adjectives.

water

wheel

This is a compound noun.

water-wheel

He gave her a five-pound box of chocolates.

This is a compound adjective.

2 Sometimes the compound word is made up of a noun or an adjective and a participle. A hyphen is used to join these.

This is a participle.

short-sighted
hard-wearing
home-made

The kind-hearted old lady gave five pots of home-made jam to the bazaar.

3 A hyphen is used to join an adjective or noun to a noun ending in d or ed.

blue-eyed

heavy-footed

She had a blue-eyed, big-eared, bird-brained boyfriend.

4 You can use a hyphen to make a group of words into an expression.

do-it-yourself

good-for-nothing

The do-it-yourself man was a bit happy-go-lucky!

5 You also use a hyphen to write numbers and fractions that are more than one word.

three-quarters
sixty-six

When she reached the age of twenty-one Cynthia inherited three-quarters of her father's money.

Nine missing... have a go!

There are nine hyphens missing. Where should they go?

The half witted taxi driver was ninety nine years old and had rather a couldn't care less attitude. This resulted in the hard working woman arriving tear stained and miserable three quarters of an hour late for the dress rehearsal.

Avoiding confusion

6 When the meaning of something is vague you can use a hyphen to avoid confusion.

> **Man eating tiger escapes from the zoo.**

> This is what is really meant.

> **Man-eating tiger escapes from the zoo.**

a walking-stick not **a walking stick**

---

7 Two words can be spelt exactly the same way and have different meanings. Sometimes a hyphen is used to make the difference clear.

recover re-cover   **resign re-sign**

She re-covered the sofa when she had recovered from her illness.

---

8 When two words are joined together and have identical letters they are separated by a hyphen.

re-echo *not* reecho

> This looks odd.

> Never write this.

grass-seed *not* grassseed

9 A hyphen can be used to attach a prefix to a word. This changes the meaning of the word.

> This is a prefix.

**pre-school
ex-army
multi-storey
anti-aircraft**

10

The man fell over-board and the ship sailed on. He sank beneath the gigan-tic waves and was never seen again.

Sometimes a word must be broken at the end of a line because it is too long to fit in completely. When this happens you can use a hyphen to divide the word.
  Try to break the word so that neither too much nor too little is left and it is still easy to read as one word.

If in doubt

Some words that were once hyphenated are now accepted as one word. If you are doubtful about when to use a hyphen always use a dictionary.

**nightdress
inkwell
haystack**

Try again

Can you see where the hyphens should go here?

Her father was an ex army officer who was injured in the war. Although he was a semi invalid he was self reliant and sat all day at his writing desk typing out novels non stop.

Apostrophes

An apostrophe looks like a comma only it is raised off the line of writing. It is used for various reasons.

1 Showing who owns what (possession)

An apostrophe goes after the owner's name to show something belongs to him or her.

> This shows the cat belongs to Jane.

If the owner is singular, put the apostrophe at the end of the word and add an "s".

This is Jane's cat.

If the word ends in an "s" already you still need an apostrophe + another "s".

That is James's dog.

When the owner is plural (more than one) and the word ends in "s" already just put the apostrophe after the "s" that is already there.

> Just the apostrophe here.

The man stole the ladies' handbags.

If the plural does not end in "s" you still add an apostrophe + "s".

> Apostrophe "s".

Take care! There is *no* apostrophe with these possessive pronouns.

He went to get the men's coats.

its	his	hers	ours	yours

2 Filling in for missing letters (contractions)

You can also use an apostrophe when you want to leave out one or more letters. The apostrophe goes in where the letters come out. In this way two words are joined together in a shorter form. These are called *contractions*.

she has	she's
you are	you're

I am	I'm	we have	we've

There are some unusual contractions.

shall not – shan't
will not – won't
I would – I'd

I had – I'd
of the clock – o'clock

Don't confuse *it's* and *its*.
it's – it is
　　　it has
its – this is the possessive pronoun.

It's time we all went to bed. (It is)

It's been a long day. (It has)

The cat wants its supper.

> There is nothing missing here.

Watch out for *who's* and *whose*. These sound the same but they are different.

Who's coming with us? (Who is)

Whose book is that? (To whom does that book belong?)

Test yourself

Where should the apostrophes go?

1. Shes got her mothers good looks, hasnt she?
2. Its the princesss birthday today, isnt it?
3. The womens Keep Fit Class opens today.

Capital letters

A capital letter should always be used for:

1 The beginning of a sentence.

> **The old lady took her dog for a walk.**

2 People's names.

> **Henrietta**   **Bert**   **Doris Smith**

> Surnames and Christian names.

3 Names of places.

> **New York**   **Mount Everest**   **River Thames**

> These can be towns, cities, countries, rivers or lakes.

But don't use capitals for the points of the compass —

> **north**   **south**   **east**   **west**

unless it is part of the name.

> **North Pole**   **South Africa**

4 Names of streets, roads and buildings.

> **Church Road**   **Main Street**
>
> **Empire State Building**

5 Titles of books, plays, songs, newspapers, films and poems.

> **The Spy Who Loved Me**   **The Mousetrap**

6 Days of the week, months of the year and for special days.

> **Monday**   **December**   **Christmas**

But capitals are not used for the seasons of the year.

> **spring   winter
> summer   autumn**

> No capitals here.

7 A capital letter is used for titles.

> **Prime Minister**   **Admiral-of-the-Fleet**

8 Also for titles before names.

> **Lord Longford**   **Prince Charles**

But these titles do not have capitals when they do not accompany a name.

> No capital here.

> **The Duke of York made a speech. Afterwards the duke walked out.**

9 The name of God, Jesus Christ and words relating to them have capitals.

> **The Messiah**   **Our Father**   **Allah**

10 The word I is always a capital. It must never be a small letter.

> **I think I am going to be sick.**

11 Capitals are always used to begin paragraphs and to start each new line of an address.

> Capitals here.

> Dr A. Giles,
> The Farthings,
> Cheam.
> Surrey.

23

Layout

Just as punctuation helps a reader to understand what you have written, the way you arrange words on a page and the amount of space you leave around them, also helps your reader to understand and take in the exact meaning of your words.

Paragraphs

Long chunks of writing unbroken by paragraphs are very offputting to most readers. A paragraph is a set of sentences. There are no hard and fast rules about how many sentences there should be in a paragraph. Use as many as makes an easily digestible piece of reading, but try to end one paragraph and begin another at a point where it is logical to have a slight break.

> The first line of a paragraph is set inwards from the margin (indented) to make it easier to see where each paragraph begins.

> Once there was a strange old man, who lived in a huge castle on the edge of a dark wood.
> He lived quite alone in his castle, but to keep him company he had hundreds of animals.

> **"Waiter, I would like my bill, please,"** said the customer.
> **"How did you find your steak, sir?"** asked the waiter.
> **"Ah, I just moved the potato and there it was."**

When you write down conversations you start a new paragraph every time one person stops speaking and another person starts. This makes it much easier for the reader to tell who is speaking which words.

When there is a complete change of subject it is usually quite easy to tell that a new paragraph is needed. If you are telling a story, the following occasions might be the right moment for a new paragraph:
1. When a person is introduced into the story.
2. When a new place is introduced into the story.
3. When there is a change of time.

Letters

There is a special pattern to follow when you write letters, which helps to make them much clearer to the reader. Below you can see one way of setting out your letters to friends or relatives.

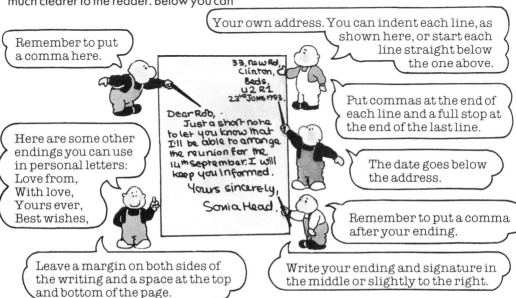

Business letters can be set out like either of the two letters below.

Write "Sir", "Madam" or "Sir/Madam" if you do not know the name of the person you are writing to.

Name and address of person you are writing to.

Your own address.

Date.

Write the person's name if you know what it is.

> 21, The Grove,
> BOCKINGFORD,
> Herts.
> E2 12C.
> 22nd May 1981.
>
> The Manager,
> Buzza Alarms Ltd,
> The Estate,
> BOXLEY,
> Kent.
> Dear Sir/Madam,
>   Please find enclosed the "Buzza" Supa Fire Alarm.
>   If you should need to contact me with regard to the repairs, then I shall be available at the above address from the 24th of this month.
>   Yours faithfully,
>   Peter Thompson.

> 21, The Grove,
> BOCKINGFORD,
> Herts,
> E2 12C
> 22nd May 1981
>
> The Manager,
> Buzza Alarms Ltd,
> The Estate,
> BOXLEY
> Kent.
> Dear Mr. King,
> Please find enclosed the "Buzza" Supa Fire Alarm.
>
> If you should need to contact me with regard to the repairs, then I shall be available at the above address from the 24th of this month.
>
> Yours sincerely,
> Peter Thompson.

Write "Yours sincerely", when you have addressed the person by name.

No capital letter for "faithfully" or "sincerely".

Write "Yours faithfully" if you have addressed the person "Dear Sir," "Dear Madam" or "Dear Sir/Madam".

1. This way of setting out a letter is known as the "fully-blocked" layout.
   The writer's address is now indented line by line.
2. Everything else including new paragraphs and the signature begin up against the left-hand margin.
3. Leave a space between paragraphs.

You can write the address on envelopes for business or personal letters in either of the two ways shown below.

The lines of the address can be indented (left) or blocked (right).

> mr.P.Thompson,
>   21, The Grove,
>   BOCKINGFORD,
>   Herts.
>   E2 12C

> mr.P. Thompson,
> 21, The Grove,
> BOCKINGFORD,
> Herts.
> E2 12C

Start the address about half-way down and half-way across the envelope.

Punctuation at the end of the lines is not essential.

Test yourself

Put in the capitals

Can you see where they should go?

There should be 19 capital letters below.

Try not to write in the book. Use paper instead.

at christmastime harriet and tom brown went to london to stay with their uncle william. their uncle was admiral-of-the-fleet in the royal navy and he had some very grand friends. while the children were staying he had a party, to which he invited the prime minister, the duke of monmouth and a famous author from america.

Apostrophes

Where should the missing apostrophes go?

1. Its the first time this week that the dog has eaten its food.
2. Toms wife is Jamess sister.
3. The ladies cloakroom is next to the mens.
4. Shes a lot older than she looks.
5. Weve not forgotten that youre an excellent cook.
6. Whose turn is it to see whos coming?

Can you shorten this conversation using apostrophes?

"I am tired," said Fred. "I have had an awful day."
"Where have you been?" asked his mother. "It is late, and we have been looking everywhere for you. You are lucky we did not call the police. I will not give you any supper until I know what is going on."

Spot the missing hyphens

There are 16 hyphens missing below. Can you see where they should go?

1. The girl with reddish brown hair kept teasing Ben, but as he was rather thick skinned and happy go lucky it didn't bother him.
2. The half witted man drove three quarters of the way in the wrong direction. He went south east instead of north west.
3. The hard working old lady had a well earned rest when she retired at the age of sixty five.
4. As her six foot tall fiancé was rather a ne'er do well, the twenty one year old girl broke off their nine month long engagement.

Colon or semi-colon?

Can you decide where to put a colon or semi-colon?

1. Many people wear uniforms to work policemen, nurses, traffic wardens, bus drivers and schoolchildren.
2. Alice never had enough to eat therefore she became thin and ill.
3. Tom worked long hours every day nevertheless he remained healthy.
4. The actor read aloud "To be, or not to be that is the question."
5. There was a knock at the door in came a tall, hooded figure.
6. At last he told us everything he had been involved in the most horrific murder.

Brackets, dashes or commas?

Can you think where to put brackets, dashes or commas to make these sentences clearer?

1. Maud took all her family three boys and three girls to the cinema.
2. They all have names beginning with the letter J Joshua, Jeremy, John, Joanne, Jessica and Jane.
3. Joanne the youngest ate three boxes of popcorn.
4. Joshua unlike the others ate nothing the whole time.
5. Poor Maud had no money left it cost £1.50 each to get in.

No punctuation at all!

Can you rewrite this conversation putting in the capital letters, full stops, commas, inverted commas, question marks, exclamation marks and anything else you think necessary?

theres a letter for you called her mother ive put it on the table
amanda rushed down the stairs tore open the envelope and
found to her delight it was an invitation
hooray ive been invited to jamess twenty first birthday party she
cried there was a pause what am i going to wear
youve got plenty of clothes dear replied her mother calmly sipping
her tea theres absolutely nothing suitable for jamess party
amanda replied it will be very smart
whats james like asked her mother suspiciously
hes six foot tall with brownish blond hair huge brown eyes and a
wonderful smile replied amanda
her mother sighed i meant what is his personality like is he hard
working trustworthy kind and clever or is he selfish and mean

Now turn over and see if you were right.

Answers

Check your brain power.

Stop the everlasting sentence (page 4)

He trudged wearily along the dusty road. His feet hurt and his head throbbed. There was not a soul in sight for miles and he wondered what to do next. Then he saw someone waving at him at the top of the hill. It was a tall man with a large hat.

Short or long? (page 5)

V.C.
etc.
Rev. J. Williams
Prof. A. Johnson
St. Augustine
cm

Automobile Association
   or Alcoholics Anynomous
Royal Automobile Club
   or Royal Armoured Corps
Young Women's Christian Association
Royal Society for the Prevention of
   Cruelty to Animals
Women's Royal Voluntary Service
Saint John, Chapter 4, verse 3
Bachelor of Science

Question quiz (page 6)

1. Where is the hotel?
2. Is it expensive?
3. Will I like the food?
4. It's a large room, isn't it?
5. How long shall I stay?

Try these (page 8)

1. The monster was huge, fat and spiky.
2. Everyone threw spears, stones, swords and boiling oil at the creature.
3. It roared, growled, spat and groaned, but still it did not die.
4. A knight appeared wearing bright, shining armour and pierced the beast with his special, magic sword.
5. The huge beast screamed, fell to the ground, rolled over and died.
6. The king rewarded the knight with gold, silver, diamonds, rubies and other precious things.

Test yourself (page 9)

1. The robber climbed through the window, crept up the stairs and peered into the bedroom.
2. She called as loudly as she could, but no-one could hear her.
3. The telephone was not far away, yet there was little she could do to reach it.
4. She quickly switched on all the lights, so the man ran away in a panic.
5. The policeman, who arrived later, told her to put a lock on her window.

Puzzle it out (page 10)

1. Inessential.
2. Inessential.
3. Essential.
4. Inessential.
5. Essential.

Comma moving puzzle (page 11)

1. The old lady collected all sorts of things: silver paper, hats, clocks and tablecloths.
   or/
   The old lady collected all sorts of things: silver, paper hats, clocks and tablecloths.
2. He had large, bright green eyes.
3. She liked Rod, who played the drums better than Jim.

Spot the mistakes (page 11)

The player(,) — not necessary.
The referee(,) — not necessary.
arms(,) — not necessary.

Turn nonsense into a conversation (page 14)

"Good morning, how are you today?" the doctor asked.
"I feel dreadful," he replied gruffly.
"You should try to get up and walk about," she suggested. "Then you might feel better."
"You must be joking!" he exclaimed. "Do you want a patient or a corpse?"

Spot the title (page 15)

1. He went to see "Superman" and "E.T." last week.
2. They had good reviews in "The Times".
3. I wanted to watch "Coronation Street" and "Dallas" so I didn't go with him.

Test yourself on brackets (page 18)

1. She got up early to go shopping (the sales were on).
2. She went with Anne (her best friend) and the lady next door.
3. It took ages to get home (there was a bus strike), and they returned exhausted.

Practise your dashes (page 19)

1. She decided to emigrate to Canada — I don't know why.
2. She packed everything she could think of — clothes, jewellery, books and records.
3. They drove on and on up the hill until at last, there to her delight was — a beautiful old house.

How well have you done?

Nine missing . . . have a go! (page 20)

The half-witted taxi-driver was ninety-nine years old and had rather a couldn't-care-less attitude. This resulted in the hard-working woman arriving tear-stained and miserable three-quarters of an hour late for the dress-rehearsal.

Try again (page 21)

Her father was an ex-army officer who was injured in the war. Although he was a semi-invalid he was self-reliant and sat all day at his writing-desk typing out novels non-stop.

Test yourself (page 22)

1. She's got her mother's good looks, hasn't she?
2. It's the princess's birthday today, isn't it?
3. The women's Keep Fit Class opens today.

Put in the capitals (page 26)

At Christmastime Harriet and Tom Brown went to London to stay with their Uncle William. Their uncle was Admiral-of-the-Fleet in the Royal Navy and he had some very grand friends. While the children were staying he had a party, to which he invited the Prime Minister, the Duke of Monmouth and a famous author from America. (19 capitals)

Apostrophes (page 26)

1. It's the first time this week that the dog has eaten its food.
2. Tom's wife is James's sister.
3. The ladies' cloakroom is next to the men's.
4. She's a lot older than she looks.
5. We've not forgotten that you're an excellent cook.
6. Whose turn is it to see who's coming?

"I'm tired," said Fred. "I've had an awful day."

"Where've you been?" asked his mother. "It's late. We've been looking everywhere for you. You're lucky we didn't call the police. I won't give you any supper until I know what's going on."

(page 26)

Spot the missing hyphens

1. The girl with reddish-brown hair kept teasing Ben, but as he was rather thick-skinned and happy-go-lucky it didn't bother him.
2. The half-witted man drove three-quarters of the way in the wrong direction. He went south-east instead of north-west.
3. The hard-working old lady had a well-earned rest when she retired at the age of sixty-five.
4. As her six-foot tall fiancé was rather a n'er-do-well, the twenty-one year old girl broke off their nine-month long engagement. (16 hyphens)

(page 27)

Colon or semi-colon?

1. Many people wear uniforms to work: policemen, nurses, traffic wardens, bus drivers and schoolchildren.
2. Alice never had enough to eat; therefore she became thin and ill.
3. Tom worked long hours every day; nevertheless he remained healthy.
4. The actor read aloud: "To be, or not to be: that is the question."
5. There was a knock at the door: in came a tall, hooded figure.
6. At last he told us everything: he had been involved in the most horrific murder.

Brackets, dashes or commas?

1. Maud took all her family – three boys and three girls – to the cinema.
2. They all have names beginning with the letter J – Joshua, Jeremy, John, Joanne, Jessica and Jane.
3. Joanne (the youngest) ate three boxes of popcorn.
4. Joshua, unlike the others, ate nothing the whole time.
5. Poor Maud had no money left (it cost £1.50 each to get in).

No punctuation at all! (page 27)

"There's a letter for you," called her mother. "I've put it on the table."

Amanda rushed down the stairs, tore open the envelope and found to her delight – it was an invitation.

"Hooray! I've been invited to James's twenty-first birthday party," she cried. There was a pause. "What am I going to wear?"

"You've got plenty of clothes, dear," replied her mother, calmly sipping her tea.

"There's absolutely nothing suitable for James's party," Amanda replied. "It will be very smart."

"What's James like?" asked her mother suspiciously.

"He's six-foot tall with brownish-blond hair, huge brown eyes and a wonderful smile," replied Amanda.

Her mother sighed. "I meant what is his personality like? Is he hard-working, trustworthy, kind and clever; or is he selfish, and mean?"

Index/glossary

adjective, 9, 20 Describing word which gives a fuller meaning to a noun: e.g. *pretty* girl, *vicious* dog.

apostrophe, 15, 22 Punctuation mark which shows: (1) that one or more letters have been missed out; e.g. didn't; (2) possession.

brackets, 18 Two punctuation marks used to enclose words or figures to separate them from the main part of the text.

capital letters, 4, 12, 23 Upper case letters used: (1) to start a sentence; (2) for proper nouns e.g. people's names.

clause, 9 Subdivision of a sentence which includes a verb. There are two kinds: (1) main clause; (2) subordinate clause. The main clause makes complete sense on its own, but a subordinate clause is dependent on the main clause for its sense: e.g. He ate a loaf of bread, (main clause) because he was hungry. (subordinate clause).

colon, 17 Mark of punctuation usually used before a quotation or contrast of ideas.

comma, 8, 9, 10, 11, 13, 16, 18 Punctuation mark representing shortest pause in a sentence.

compound word, 20 Word made up from two or more other words.

conjunction, 9, 17 Word which connects words, clauses or sentences.

contraction, 22 Shortened form of two words, using an apostrophe.

dash, 19 Punctuation mark which marks a pause or break in the sense of the text.

direct question, 6 The kind of question which expects an answer in return.

direct speech, 12 The exact words that someone speaks.

exclamation mark, 4, 7 Punctuation mark used at the end of a sentence or phrase, when the content conveys a strong feeling or emotion.

full stop, 4, 5, 16, 18 Strongest punctuation mark making the most definite pause. Used at the end of all sentences which are not questions or exclamations.

hyphen, 20, 21 Punctuation mark used to link two or more words together to make one word or expression.

indirect question, 6 This kind of sentence does not ask a question but tells you what question was asked.

inverted commas, 12, 13, 14, 15 Punctuation marks used to show the exact words that someone has spoken.

noun, 4, 20 Word used as the name of a person, thing or place: e.g. dog, man.

paragraph, 23, 24 Passage or section of writing marked off by indenting the first line.

parenthesis, 18 Another word for brackets. Words inside brackets are also called parenthesis.

participle, 20 Part of verb. Can be past or present. (1) Present participle is part of verb that usually ends in *ing*: e.g. making, laughing, working; (2) past participle is the part of the verb which follows "have" or "has" in the past tense: e.g. They have *eaten*. He has *made* it.

phrase, 10 Small group of words without a verb, which is not a complete sentence.

prefix, 21 Small addition to a word made by joining on one or more letters at the beginning. e.g. ex, pre, anti.

pronoun, 22 Word which stands instead of a noun. There are many kinds of pronoun including *possessive* pronouns (mine, yours, hers).

question marks, 4, 6 Punctuation mark used at the end of a sentence which asks a question.

quotation, 4, 14, 16 One or more words or sentences borrowed from another piece of text.

reported speech, 12 Repeating or "reporting" in your own words what someone has said.

semi-colon, 16 Punctuation mark indicating a longer pause than a comma, but less than a colon or full stop.

sentences, 4, 9 A word or group of words which make complete sense on their own.

subordinate, 9 (see clause).

verb, 4 Word which shows some kind of action or being: e.g. run, jump, think, is, was, were.

verb of saying, 13 Verb which is another way of expressing "says" or "said" depending on the context: e.g. whisper, mutter, etc. Usually comes before or after speech in inverted commas: e.g. "Who are you?" she *asked*.

First published in 1983 by Usborne Publishing Ltd, Usborne House, 83-85 Saffron Hill, London EC1N 8RT, England.

© 1990, 1983 Usborne Publishing

 Printed in Portugal

ENGLISH SPELLING

English Spelling: Contents

With thanks to Diccon Swan for his help and advice.

Why English spelling is difficult

English is used in many parts of the world as a first or second language, yet it is a very difficult language to learn.

There seems to be no logical pattern as to the way English words are spelt, and the way the words are pronounced often does not help either.

The reason why English is such an extraordinary language is that it is a mixture of many other languages.

More recently, our language has been influenced by the two World Wars and by American films and culture.

It is fun to discover where words came from. The study of word derivations is called *etymology.* Most good dictionaries provide a certain amount of information on etymology, but if you want a lot of detail you will need a special *etymological dictionary.*

Where do the words come from?

Long ago the British Isles were invaded by many different races, and each of these races contributed words to the language we now speak.

The Ancient Britons spoke a language called Celtic. Then Britain was invaded by the Romans who brought with them the Roman alphabet which we use today.

When Roman power declined, Britain was invaded by the Jutes, the Saxons and the Angles. Eventually their languages mingled to form Anglo/Saxon which is really the basis of the English language.

Next came the Viking invasions which introduced Scandinavian words; and finally there was the Norman Conquest which was very important as it introduced French into the language.

Over the centuries words from many other countries were gradually introduced into English as merchants travelled across the world, and scholars were influenced by the Renaissance. Latin and Greek were used by educated people, and for more than a century Latin was the only language recognized in English schools.

The British ruled in India for two hundred years and many Indian words have been absorbed into English from there.

These words came from India.

thug **verandah** **bungalow**

Stories about words

In Roman times each Roman soldier was given an allowance to pay for the salt he needed. The Latin word for salt is sal. Nowadays there is an English word meaning "wages paid by the month or by the year". Do you know what it is?[1]

During the Middle Ages in England the pilgrims going to Canterbury used to ride at a gentle gallop known as the "Canterbury gallop". There is now a six-letter word to describe this gallop. Can you think what that is?[2]

There are lots of stories about words. See if you can discover some more.

Words from names

Some of the words we use now are connected with the names of people or places.

Sardines are so called because they are caught off the shores of Sardinia.

Wellington boots are named after the 1st Duke of Wellington who wore very high boots covering his knees.

The 4th Earl of Sandwich was an English nobleman who loved hunting. One day he hunted for twenty-four hours without stopping, and the only food he ate was meat placed between slices of bread. Food eaten like this has been called after him ever since.

[1]salary [2]canter

How we spell

The first thing usually learnt at school is the alphabet. The English alphabet is made up of twenty-six letters. Five of these letters are called vowels — a e i o u. The other twenty-one letters are called consonants — b c d f g h j k l m n p q r s t v w x y z. The letter y can act as a consonant or a vowel depending on its position in a word.

| yacht | happy |

Here it is a consonant.

Here it is a vowel.

Every word has a vowel letter in it. Try to remember this when you are writing.

Sounds

Each vowel letter has a short and long sound. (The long sound is the name of the letter.)

| c**a**t   p**e**n   d**i**g   l**o**g   t**u**b |

These are short vowel sounds.

| m**a**ne   th**e**se   t**i**de   h**o**me   t**u**be |

These are long vowel sounds.

The dictionary shows you which are short or long sounds by using special marks.*

Some words are easy to spell because each letter stands for a sound.

c-a-t spells cat.

This is easy.

Letters can, however, be combined in different ways to make many sounds.

| ea   oa   ee   ou   ch   sh   th   ck |

Some letter combinations make the same sound.

| oi   oy   ea   ee |

This is when it becomes tricky. Many words or parts of words *sound* the same but are spelt differently.

| pain pane | buoy boy |

*See page 39

Sometimes the combination of letters may *look* the same but *sound* different.

| enough | though |

These are things which you have to look out for and try to remember.

Syllables

Words are made up of one or more syllables. These are one syllable words:

| pen   hat   pig   fat |

These words are more than one syllable:

| better | sister | wonderful |

When you speak, you stress different syllables in different words. Most dictionaries will show you which syllable in the word is to be stressed most.

Here the stress is on the first syllable.

Here the stress is on the second syllable.

| mas'-ter | mis-take' |

ba-na-na

Some people misspell words because they miss out syllables. When you are not sure how to spell a long word try to sound every syllable as you write.

The pronunciation of words laid out in most dictionaries, and in this book, is the standard one (without any accent) and does not attempt to deal with regional accents in any way.

Rules

There are certain spelling rules to help you learn English spelling. Unfortunately, there are so many exceptions to the rules that you wonder whether it is worth learning them in the first place. However, it is better to have some guide than no guide at all. In this book, the rules are laid out as simply and as clearly as possible to provide the guidelines. The rules have pink boxes round them to make them easy to spot.

35

Using a dictionary

If you want to improve your spelling it is very important to have a good dictionary, and to try to look up words whenever you are in doubt about how they are spelt.

Besides telling you how to spell a word, a dictionary tells you a lot of other things. It tells you what a word means, how to use it, where it came from and how to say it. All this information has to be squashed into as small a space as possible. To do this the people who write dictionaries use abbreviations, signs and symbols, and different kinds of type which helps to make things clearer.

Different dictionaries use slightly different symbols and abbreviations, so look in the front of your own dictionary to find an explanation of the code.

Below is an entry from the *Concise Oxford Dictionary*. The labels around it tell you what everything stands for and should help you to decode your own dictionary.

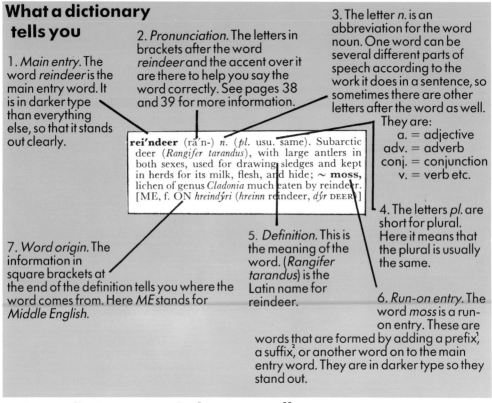

What a dictionary tells you

1. *Main entry*. The word *reindeer* is the main entry word. It is in darker type than everything else, so that it stands out clearly.

2. *Pronunciation*. The letters in brackets after the word *reindeer* and the accent over it are there to help you say the word correctly. See pages 38 and 39 for more information.

3. The letter *n*. is an abbreviation for the word noun. One word can be several different parts of speech according to the work it does in a sentence, so sometimes there are other letters after the word as well. They are:

    a. = adjective
    adv. = adverb
    conj. = conjunction
    v. = verb etc.

rei'ndeer (rā'n-) *n.* (*pl.* usu. same). Subarctic deer (*Rangifer tarandus*), with large antlers in both sexes, used for drawing sledges and kept in herds for its milk, flesh, and hide; ~ **moss,** lichen of genus *Cladonia* much eaten by reindeer. [ME, f. ON *hreindýri* (*hreinn* reindeer, *dýr* DEER)]

7. *Word origin*. The information in square brackets at the end of the definition tells you where the word comes from. Here *ME* stands for *Middle English*.

5. *Definition*. This is the meaning of the word. (*Rangifer tarandus*) is the Latin name for reindeer.

4. The letters *pl.* are short for plural. Here it means that the plural is usually the same.

6. *Run-on entry*. The word *moss* is a run-on entry. These are words that are formed by adding a prefix,[1] a suffix,[2] or another word on to the main entry word. They are in darker type so they stand out.

Using a dictionary to help you spell

How can you find out how to spell a word by using a dictionary? First of all you make a guess at the spelling and check to see if you are right. If you are wrong, make another guess and try again. Here are some useful hints to help you find the word you want.

1 All dictionaries have words listed in alphabetical order. The words are arranged firstly according to the letter they begin with. When two words begin with the *same* letter they are arranged alphabetically according to the second letter; and so on.

If a long word has the same first letters as a short word, but just goes on further, the short word always comes first.

latch before match — l before m.

match before meat — a before e.

medal before melon — d before l.

36

[1]See page 50. [2]See page 52.

2

In English, one sound can be spelt in many different ways. If your first guess is wrong and you are trying to think of another sensible guess, it might help you to turn to page 40. This suggests alternative ways in which the consonant sounds in your words might be spelt. If this does not help, look at pages 42 and 43 to see in what other ways the vowel sounds in your word may be spelt.

Here are some guesses you might make about how to spell "enough".

enuf	inough
enuff	enugh
enouph	enogh
enough	enouf

3

Some words have double letters where you don't expect them. Look out for these. You cannot always hear the difference between a double or single consonant sound, and so you can be caught out when you try to spell it. (See pages 40, 52 and 53 for guidelines to help you.)

This one is right.

unneccessary
unneccesary
unnecessary
uneccessary
unecesarry

4

Sometimes you may not be able to find the word you want because it contains a letter which is not pronounced, so you cannot hear it when you say the word. Letters which are not pronounced are called silent letters. They can be anywhere in a word. If you are having difficulty finding a word, turn to page 41 to help you decide whether it might contain a silent letter.

To look a word up it is very important to know what letter it starts with.

gnaw
honest
know
psalm
wrong

5

You may not find the exact word you are looking for as a main entry. Many words are formed by adding different endings, or "suffixes" (see page 52), to main entry words. If adding a suffix to a word alters the spelling in a way you would not expect, the spelling of the word plus its suffix may be listed in the run-on entries.

descending
descended
descends

Look up under "descend".

6

Some words consist of two other words joined together. They may be joined by a small mark called a hyphen, or simply written as one word. If you cannot find a word like this when you look it up, try looking it up in the run-on entries under the first part of the word. If this does not work, check the run-on entries under the second part of the word.

bookworm
song-thrush
ant-eater

Looking-up checklist

If you can't find a word in the dictionary, try:

1. Checking the consonant sounds on page 40 for for alternative spellings.

2. Checking the vowel sounds on pages 42 and 43 for alternative spellings.

3. Checking for silent letters on page 41.

Pronunciation and spelling

It is very important when learning to spell a word to say it aloud to yourself, so that your mind links the sound of the word and the feeling of saying it with the look of the word on paper and the feeling of writing it down. On this page and the one opposite are some suggestions on how you can make your pronunciation help your spelling.

1

If you come across a word you are not sure how to spell, it is often a good idea to break it up into *syllables* or sounds. A syllable is a part of a word pronounced as a single sound. It can form a complete word, or be part of a larger word and it usually consists of a vowel sound with or without consonants. When you split the word up into these separate sounds and say them slowly and clearly, you will often find that you feel more confident about spelling them right. This works well for words that are spelt more or less as they sound.

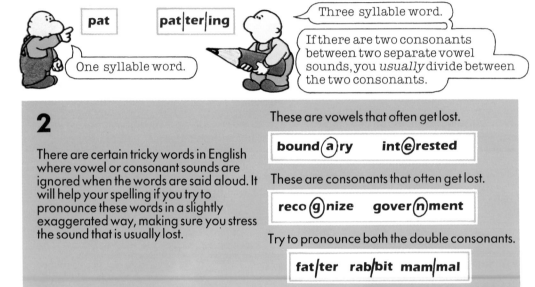

pat

pat|ter|ing

One syllable word.

Three syllable word.

If there are two consonants between two separate vowel sounds, you *usually* divide between the two consonants.

2

There are certain tricky words in English where vowel or consonant sounds are ignored when the words are said aloud. It will help your spelling if you try to pronounce these words in a slightly exaggerated way, making sure you stress the sound that is usually lost.

These are vowels that often get lost.

bound(a)ry   int(e)rested

These are consonants that often get lost.

reco(g)nize   gover(n)ment

Try to pronounce both the double consonants.

fat|ter rab|bit mam|mal

3

For words in which the pronunciation and the spelling seem to have little connection with each other, it is quite a good idea to have your own private way of pronouncing them to help you with the spelling. This can be very useful for words that have a silent letter in them.

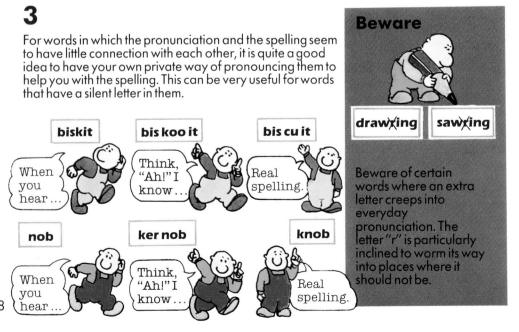

biskit

When you hear ...

bis koo it

Think, "Ah!" I know ...

bis cu it

Real spelling.

nob

When you hear ...

ker nob

Think, "Ah!" I know ...

knob

Real spelling.

Beware

draw~~r~~ing   **saw~~r~~ing**

Beware of certain words where an extra letter creeps into everyday pronunciation. The letter "r" is particularly inclined to worm its way into places where it should not be.

How a dictionary helps with pronunciation

1

If you are not sure how to pronounce a word correctly, a dictionary can be very helpful. A good dictionary will show how words are normally spoken, by using a system of signs and symbols. Pronunciation can, of course, vary from one region or country to another.

Radio and TV have helped to establish a standard or "received" pronunciation.

Dictionaries give what is called "received pronunciation". This is what most people would recognize as "good English".

2

Most dictionaries give a pronunciation guide for vowels, consonants and certain groups of letters, in the introduction. For words that present particular difficulties a dictionary often gives a respelling of the whole word, or just the difficult bit, in brackets after the word. The respelling is given in "phonetic" spelling based on a phonetic alphabet. A phonetic alphabet is a special kind of alphabet in which each letter, symbol or group of letters always represents the same sound, so that there is no confusion about what sound is written down. The phonetic system used by the dictionary should also be explained in the introduction.

conscientious (-shĭĕnshus)

Phonetic system:

sh = **sh as in ship**
ĭ = **i as in bit**
ĕ = **e as in net**
n = **n as in net**
u = **u as in bonus**
s = **s as in sip**

Most phonetic systems stay as close as possible to the normal alphabet.

3

Each of the five vowels in the alphabet can be pronounced in many different ways. Most dictionaries use a system of marks over vowels to help show the correct pronunciation. The key to these marks should appear in the explanation of the phonetic system in the introduction.

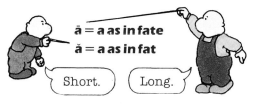

ā = **a as in fate**
ă = **a as in fat**

Short. Long.

4

In long words, one or more of the syllables usually has more stress or emphasis on it than the others. Dictionaries normally show which is the most strongly sounded syllable by putting an accent, a comma or a stop after the stressed syllable. Some dictionaries divide their main entry words into syllables.

co'nsonant
a'lphabet
vow'el

Beware

Be careful with the spelling of these two words:

I *pronounce* words clearly.

But

My *pronunciation* is clear.

No "o" here.

What is the real spelling?

These words are written according to their phonetic spelling in the *Concise Oxford Dictionary*. Do you know how each of them is really spelt?

1. āk   6. prĕ'shus
2. bihāvyer 7. ka'rĭj
3. bĭ'znis   8. sĭ'zerz
4. for'ĭn   9. stŭ'mak
5. nŏ'lij   10. hăng'kerchĭf

Consonant sounds

Many sounds in English can be spelt in different ways. Below is a chart showing the consonant sounds that can be spelt in several ways and the different ways of spelling them. If you are having difficulty spelling a word or finding it in the dictionary, you may find it useful to look up the sound you want in this chart.

F The sound "f" as in *fall* can be spelt:

1. "f" as in *frog*
2. "ff" as in *giraffe*
3. "gh" as in *laugh*
4. "ph" as in *pheasant*

G The sound "g" as in *grab* can be spelt:

1. "g" as in *goat*
2. "gg" as in *egg*
3. "gh" as in *ghost*
4. "gu" as in *guitar*

J The sound "j" as in *jog* can be spelt:

1. "dg" as in *fudge*
2. "g" as in *giant*
3. "j" as in *joke*

K The sound "k" as in *kill* can be spelt:

1. "c" as in *cat*
2. "cc" as in *accordion*
3. "ch" as in *echo*
4. "ck" as in *duck*
5. "k" as in *king*
6. "qu" as in *bouquet*
7. "que" as in *cheque*

S The sound "s" as in *salute* can be spelt:

1. "ce" as in *mice*
2. "s" as in *snake*
3. "sc" as in *scent*
4. "ss" as in *hiss*

SH The sound "sh" as in *shoot* can be spelt:

1. "ch" as in *machine*
2. "ci" as in *special*
3. "s" as in *sugar*
4. "sh" as in *shampoo*
5. "si" as in *pension*
6. "ssi" as in *mission*
7. "ss" as in *pressure*
8. "ti" as in *nation*

Z The sound "z" as in *zoom* can be spelt:

1. "s" as in *daisy*
2. "z" as in *lazy*

Hard and soft "c"s and "g"s

The letters "c" and "g" can be either soft (*cinema, giant*) or hard (*card, gap*). The soft "g" sounds like a "j"; the soft "c" sounds like an "s". Both letters are only soft when they are followed by an "e", an "i" or a "y".

gem	**gin**	**gym**
garden	**gum**	**good**

celery	**cider**	**cycle**
cactus	**corn**	**cucumber**

Double letters

It is often difficult to hear any difference in sound between a single or double consonant. One useful guideline is to think about the sound of the vowel before it. *Double* consonants in the middle of a word *usually* only appear after a *short* vowel sound.*

These are all short vowel sounds.

matter
poppy
puppy

These are all long vowel sounds.

later
pony
pupil

*See pages 35 and 42.

Silent letters

English words are full of silent letters. These letters are not pronounced but must always be written.

You may wonder why these silent letters are there in the first place. The answer is that they used to be pronounced. In the Middle Ages all the consonants and most of the silent "s"s were still being sounded. Gradually, as pronunciation changed, some of the letters became silent.

Here are some examples of silent letters and words containing them.

Collecting words with silent letters

If you have a spelling notebook, it is a good idea to make a collection of words with silent letters. Use a different page for each separate silent letter and add words as you come across them.

Silent W
wr   wh
wren   whoever
wrinkle   wholewheat
wriggle   whom

B (after "m")
lamb   bomb
thumb   comb

(before "t")
debt   subtle

E An "e" on the end of a word is not usually pronounced. Many words have a silent "e" on the end.
The silent "e" usually makes the previous vowel long, if there is only one consonant between it and the previous vowel:

hat   hate

G (always before "n")
gnat   gnome   sign

GH (at the end of a word)
weigh   though

(before "t")
bright   daughter

H (at the beginning of a word)
honest   hour   heir

(after "r")
rhubarb
rhyme
rhinoceros

(after "w" – in some accents, such as Scottish, you can hear an "h" when it comes after a "w")
whip
whisky

K (always before "n")
knot   knee   knife

L
half   calm   talk

N (after "m")
autumn   solemn
hymn   condemn

P (always before "s", "n" or "t". These words come from Greek)
pneumatic
pneumonia
psalm
psychology
pterodactyl

R Sometimes "r" is not pronounced at the end of a word unless the next word begins with a vowel:
far   far enough

S
island   aisle

T (usually after "s")
whistle
castle
listen
rustle

(it is also hard to hear a "t" before "ch")
watch
fetch
itch

W (before "r")
wrong   write

(sometimes before "h")
who   whole

Vowel sounds

1 There are five vowels in the English alphabet. Each of these vowel letters, a e i o u, has two sounds:

a. A short sound:

| man hop pip tub pet |

b. A long sound:

| mane hope pipe tube Pete |

2 Dictionaries usually show which are short or long vowel sounds by putting different marks above the vowel letter to show you how to pronounce it.

| hăd |
| băd |
| lĭp |

This is the sign for a short vowel.

| shīne |
| hāte |
| tūne |

This is the sign for a long vowel.

3 You can make more vowel sounds by writing two or more vowels together, or by writing a vowel and a consonant together.

| boar   pier |

Two vowels.

| new   half   bird |

A vowel and a consonant.

Sounds chart

There are about 20 vowel sounds altogether in English and this chart shows you the most common ways of spelling them.

The sound "a" as in *hat* is nearly always spelt with an "a".

The sound "a" as in *skate* can be spelt:
1. "a" as in *gate*
2. "ai" as in *plain*
3. "ay" as in *crayon*
4. "ea" as in *steak*
5. "ei" as in *eight*
6. "ey" as in *grey*

The sound "a" as in *vase* can be spelt:
1. "a" as in *pass*
2. "al" as in *half*
3. "ar" as in *car*
4. "au" as in *laugh*

The sound "air" as in *fair* can be spelt:
1. "air" as in *chair*
2. "are" as in *share*
3. "ear" as in *bear*
4. "ere" as in *there*
5. "eir" as in *their*

The sound "aw" as in *yawn* can be spelt:
1. "a" as in *ball*
2. "al" as in *walk*
3. "augh" as in *caught*
4. "aw" as in *law*
5. "oar" as in *roar*
6. "or" as in *sword*
7. "ough" as in *ought*

The sound "e" as in *spell* can be spelt:
1. "e" as in *bed*
2. "ea" as in *bread*

The sound "ear" as in *disappear* can be spelt:
1. "ear" as in *dear*
2. "eer" as in *beer*
3. "ere" as in *here*
4. "ier" as in *pier*

Can you think of more ways of spelling these sounds?

The sound "ee" as in *see* can be spelt:
1. "e" as in *demon*
2. "ea" as in *eat*
3. "ee" as in *keen*
4. "ei" as in *ceiling*
5. "ey" as in *key*
6. "i" as in *sardine*
7. "ie" as in *field*

the sound "er" as in *jerk* can be spelt:
1. "er" as in *earn*
2. "er" as in *service*
3. "ir" as in *bird*
4. "or" as in *word*
5. "our" as in *journey*
6. "ur" as in *nurse*

The sound "i" as in *sit* can be spelt:
1. "i" as in *pin*
2. "ui" as in *build*
3. "y" as in *pyramid*

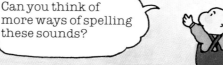

The "i" before "e" rule

One of the vowel sounds that people most frequently get wrong is the "ee" sound. Here is a rule to help you..

"i" before "e" except after "c" when the sound is "ee".

 These are "i" before "e" words.

achieve	field
believe	grief
brief	piece
chief	shield
thief	siege

| ceiling |
| deceive |
| conceit |
| receive |
| perceive |

 These are "e" before "i" words.

The most common exceptions to this rule are: seize, weir, weird.

Y as a vowel

The letter "y" is sometimes used as a vowel depending on its position in a word. When it is placed at the beginning of a word it usually acts as a consonant. If it is at the end of a word, or if it has an "i" sound, it acts as a vowel.

Here it is a vowel.

yoyo   yacht

Wye valley

The sound "i" as in *drive* can be spelt:
1. "i" as in *dime*
2. "igh" as in *high*
3. "ie" as in *pie*
4. "ye" as in *goodbye*
5. "y" as in *cry*

the sound "o" as in *hop* can be spelt:
1. "a" as in *wasp*
2. "au" as in *sausage*
3. "o" as in *blot*
4. "ou" as in *cough*

The sound "o" as in *poke* can be spelt:
1. "o" as in *bone*
2. "oa" as in *soap*
3. "oe" as in *toe*
4. "ow" as in *blow*

The sound "ow" as in *frown* can be spelt:
1. "ou" as in *cloud*
2. "ow" as in *clown*

The sound "oy" as in *boy* can be spelt:
1. "oi" as in *coin*
2. "oy" as in *toy*

The sound "u" as in *duck* can be spelt:
1. "o" as in *come*
2. "ou" as in *young*
3. "u" as in *much*

The sound "u" as in *push* can be spelt:
1. "oo" as in *book*
2. "ou" as in *would*
3. "u" as in *bull*

The sound "u" as in *rule* can be spelt:
1. "ew" as in *screw*
2. "o" as in *do*
3. "oo" as in *shoot*
4. "ou" as in *soup*
5. "u" as in *flute*
6. "ui" as in *fruit*

The sound "u" ("you") as in *use* can be spelt:
1. "ew" as in *new*
2. "u" as in *duty*

The words above have a "y" sound in front of the "u".

The sound "ore" as in *more* can be spelt:
1. "oor" as in *poor*
2. "our" as in *tour*
3. "ur" as in *jury*
4. "ure" as in *sure*

Make a list of any more words that have this sound.

43

Words which sound alike HOMOPHONES

There are many words which sound alike but are spelt differently. Words that sound alike are called *homophones*. (The word homophone means "the same sound".) You will come across a great many *pairs* of homophones, but you will also find some groups of three or more words with the same sound but different meanings and spellings. Try to spot homophones and make a list of which spelling goes with which meaning.

This is a prefix* which means "the same".

read   reed

boy   buoy

Try these

Here are ten sets of the most common homophones. Can you fit them into the sentences correctly?

1. hear/here	1. "Come over . . . . . ," called Fred, but Alice was so busy she didn't . . . . .
2. new/knew	2. No-one . . . . . the people who had moved into the . . . . . house.
3. no/know	3. ". . . . . , I don't . . . . . the answer to your question.
4. past/passed	4. The girl . . . . . out as her favourite pop star went . . . . .
5. right/write	5. Most people . . . . . with their . . . . . hand.
6. weather/whether	6. Even the . . . . . man couldn't tell . . . . . it was going to be wet or fine.
7. which/witch	7. The silly . . . . . forgot . . . . . spell to use.
8. wood/would	8. He told us he . . . . . be moving to a house on the edge of a . . . . .
9. where/wear	9. She didn't know . . . . . they were going, or what she should . . . . .
10. to/too/two	10. . . . . . of the boys were . . . . . young . . . . . go . . . . . the football match.

Apostrophe muddle

Apostrophes are often used to make two words into one. When this happens the word formed can sometimes sound like another word. Make sure you do not confuse the words on the left below with their sound-alike words on the right.

On the end of another word.

they're (they are)	– there their
it's (it is, it has)	– its
you're (you are)	– your
who's (who is)	– whose
've (have)	– of

These words are all possessive adjectives – they show that something belongs to something else.

44

*See pages 50 and 51.

Nouns and verbs which sound alike

Do you know the difference between these pairs of words?

practise	practice
advise	advice
license	licence

You can *hear* the difference between the verb "advise" and the noun "advice". Remember how to spell these words and it will help you with others like them.

The words on the left are verbs; the ones on the right are nouns. Look at the examples below to see how they are used.

**I practise my piano playing every day.
I need more practice at using the pedals.**

The verbs are spelt with an "s". The nouns are spelt with a "c".

**I advise you to be more careful.
I always give you good advice.**

**I am licensed to drive a car.
I have lost my driving licence.**

Meter or metre?

A "meter" is an instrument that measures something like gas, electricity, water or parking.

A speedometer measures speed.

A thermometer measures temperature.

A "metre" is a unit of length. The ending "metre" is used for all lengths based on the metre: kilometre, centimetre and millimetre.

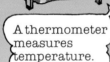

The Americans use the word "meter" where the English use "metre". Don't let this confuse you.

Puns

A pun is a saying or sentence which makes use of homophones in a funny or clever way. Newspaper headlines, advertising slogans and some jokes and riddles are often puns.

Teacher: "No fighting allowed in here!"

Pupil: "We weren't fighting aloud sir, we were fighting quietly."

"Have you heard the story about the peacock? . . . It's a beautiful tale (tail)."

Spot the mistakes

There are 13 mistakes in the sentences below. Can you find them all?

1. Cynthia had such a pane in her heal it maid her grown.
2. Fred was so greedy he ate a hole current cake without offering anyone else a peace.
3. Tom had such huge mussels he could lift too cars with his bear hands.
4. The drunkard spent the night in a prison sell and was find for using fowl language.

Plurals

A singular word is a word which refers to one thing or group of things; a plural word refers to more than one thing. When singular words become plural they change their spelling slightly to show the difference in their meaning. The way they change depends on what letter they end with in the singular.

The plural of most words is formed by adding "s" to the singular.

Words ending in hissing sounds

s, sh, tch, x, z

Words ending in "s" and other hissing sounds such as "sh", "tch", "x" and "z" take "es" to form the plural.

dress	dresses
dish	dishes
match	matches
box	boxes
waltz	waltzes

+es

If you try to say these words in the plural by just adding an "s", you will see why you need to add an "e" before the "s".

Words ending in "ch" take "es" if the "ch" has a soft sound.

church
churches

Here you don't need an "e" to make the plural sound different from the singular.

If the "ch" has a hard sound, like a "k", you just add "s".

monarch
monarchs

If the hissing sound is followed by an "e", you just add an "s".

rose
roses

Test yourself

Can you change all these words into the plural using the above rules to help you?

1. address	7. lash	13. tax
2. garden	8. princess	14. table
3. case	9. pitch	15. arch
4. loss	10. dish	16. house
5. wish	11. ship	17. torch
6. march	12. crash	18. splash

Words ending in "y"

> If there is a vowel before the "y", just add "s" to form the plural.
>
> If there is a consonant before the "y" change the "y" to "i" and add "es".

Singular ➡	**Plural**	**Singular** ➡	**Plural**
vowel + y	+ s	consonant + y	+ ies
boy	boys	puppy	puppies

Any kind of name ending in "y" takes "s" in the plural, even if there is a consonant before the "y", so that the name will not be changed.

"Do you know Mr and Mrs Henry?"
"Yes, I know the Henrys."

Helpful hint! Pick on a word ending in "y", whose plural you already know, e.g. boy (boys). From this you can easily work out that it must be consonant + y that ends in "ies".

Add the right ending

Can you make these "y" words plural?

1. toy
2. misery
3. donkey
4. deputy
5. country
6. quay
7. memory
8. jelly
9. tray
10. robbery

Words ending in "o"

Most words ending in "o" make their plural by adding "s".

piano   pianos

But here are some words that end in "oes" in the plural. There is no rule to help you to tell which words end in "oes"; you just have to try to remember them.

There are also some words that can end in either "os" or "oes". You cannot go wrong with these. Use whichever ending you think looks best.

Try to remember these words.

buffalo**es**
cargo**es**
domino**es**
echo**es**
hero**es**
mosquito**es**
potato**es**
tomato**es**

Eskimos or Eskimoes
flamingos or flamingoes
halos or haloes
mementos or mementoes
mottos or mottoes
zeros or zeroes

47

Words ending in "f", "fe" and "ff"

Most words drop the "f", or "fe", and add "ves" in the plural.

| leaf |
| leaves |

If you say them aloud you can always hear which words end in "ves".

A few words just add "s" to form the plurals.

dwarfs	proofs
chiefs	roofs
griefs	beliefs

Take your pick.

Four words can be spelt either "fs" or "ves".

hoofs	hooves
turfs	turves
scarfs	scarves
wharfs	wharves

Which of these pairs are wrong?

Only some of these pairs of words have the correct plural. Can you pick out the *wrong* ones?

1. chief chiefs
2. roof roofs
3. scarf scarves
4. calf calfs
5. sheriff sheriffs
6. knife knifes
7. leaf leafs
8. wife wives
9. proof proofs
10. half halves
11. tariff tariffs
12. life lives
13. shelf shelfs
14. wolf wolves
15. elf elfs
16. wharf wharves
17. grief griefs
18. cliff cliffs
19. gulf gulves
20. mischief mischiefs
21. loaf loafs
22. belief believes

Words with hyphens

Hyphenated nouns add an "s" to the main noun part.

| son-in-law |
| sons-in-law |

"Sons" is the most important part.

But where the nouns are formed from verbs, add an "s" on the end.

| lay-by |
| lay-bys |

"Lay" is part of a verb.

Words that stay the same

Sometimes the plural stays the same as the singular.

sheep	sheep
deer	deer
aircraft	aircraft

Complete change

Some words change their spelling completely in the plural.

mouse	mice
woman	women
tooth	teeth

Can you think of any more?

Latin words

Some words, which have kept their Latin form, take Latin plural endings.

Words ending in "us" change to "i" in the plural.

terminus	termini

Words ending in "a" change to "ae" in the plural.

formula	formulae

Words ending in "um" change to "a" in the plural.

medium	media

Words ending in "is" change to "es" in the plural.

axis	axes

Puzzle it out

What is the plural of:

1. antenna
2. cargo
3. axis
4. salmon
5. motto
6. brother-in-law
7. woman
8. buffalo
9. goose
10. piano
11. tomato
12. man-of-war

Use all the information to help you.

What is the singular of:

1. leaves
2. holidays
3. radishes
4. patches
5. echoes
6. kangaroos
7. courts-martial
8. opportunities
9. cities
10. hippopotami
11. abscesses
12. oases

Spot the mistakes

There are 13 mistakes in the story below. Can you spot them all?

One day the Kennedies went out for a walk, taking with them their dog and its two puppys. They wanted to get away from the noise of the cars, lorrys and busess; so they headed towards the open fields.

The leafs on the trees rustled in the breeze and the sun shone down on the rooves of the houses. As they drew nearer to the countryside, the dog chased butterflys and the puppys yapped at some donkies which were peering through the bushs.

At last the family reached the river and sat down to eat their picnic lunchs. Unfortunately, as they ate some tomatos they were attacked by a swarm of mosquitos.

49

Adding to the beginning of words

A prefix is a group of letters which can be added on to the front of other words to change their meaning. Prefixes have their own meanings (they usually come from Latin and Greek words), which become part of the meaning of the new word. If you know the meaning and spelling of some of the most common prefixes, it can help you to work out the meaning and spelling of a great many of the words we use.

"Pre" is a prefix. It means before.

A prefix is something you fix before another word.

Most dictionaries list prefixes as main entry words and give their meanings.

Here are some of the more common prefixes with their meanings:

appear

re

ab-	away, from	per-	through, thorough
ad-	to, into	poly-	many
ante-	before	post-	after
anti-	against	pro- ⎫	in favour of,
com-	with, together	pur- ⎬	forwards, in front
de-	down, below, off		onwards,
dia-	through, across	re-	again, back
en- ⎫	in	sub-	below
in- ⎬		super- ⎫	over, beyond
epi-	upon, above	sur- ⎬	
ex-	out, away	syn-	with, together
hyper-	above, greater	tele-	far away
hypo-	below, lesser		
inter-	between	uni-	one
		bi-	two
mal-	bad	tri-	three

Opposite meanings

A prefix is often added to give the opposite meaning to a word. All the prefixes on the right give the meaning of "not", "opposite of", "without". They are called *negative* prefixes.

dis-	non-
in-	un-
mis-	

Test 1   Can you add the right prefixes to the words below?

dis or de	*dis or mis*	*ante or anti*
part	take	natal
agreement	understanding	septic
lay	please	climax
obedient	satisfied	chamber
im or il	*un or in*	*pre or pro*
legal	discreet	ceed
moral	reliable	pare
logical	expensive	caution
possible	important	vide

Remember this rule

The rule about spelling words with prefixes is quite easy to remember:

> You do not change the spelling of a word when adding a prefix to it.

dis + solve = dissolve

Even when the last letter of the prefix is the same as the first letter of the word you are adding it to, don't miss out any letters.

mis + spell = misspell

You need both "s"s here.

All and well are exceptions

When you add "all" or "well" to the front of other words, they only have one "l".

all + together = altogether

well + come = welcome

All's well, if there's only one "l".

Prefixes in disguise

Do these words have prefixes?

arrange	collect	suffer
illegal	irregular	suppose

Many words in common use have prefixes that you might not recognize as prefixes. This is because some prefixes which end in a consonant change according to the word they are attached to — usually to make them easier to pronounce. The last letter of the prefix normally changes to become the same as the first letter of the base word:

ad- can become ac-, af-, ag-, al-, an-, ap-, ar-, as-, at-

com- can become col-, cor-, con-

in- can become il-, im-, ir-

sub- can become suc-, suf-, sug-, sup-, sur-, sus-

Test 2 What does the prefix in front of each of these words mean?

*ad*vance
*de*scend
*super*vise
*bi*lingual
*sub*merge
*mal*formation
*en*trance
*ex*it

Test 3 Can you make these words opposite in meaning by adding a negative prefix?

employment
fortune
respectful
pleasant
appear
responsible
alcoholic
patient

Adding to the end of words

A suffix is a letter or group of letters added to the end of a word to change the way you use it.

When you add a suffix to a word it shows the way in which the word is used and can change it from one part of speech to another.

end **-ing**

She sat dream*ing* all day long. (verb)

This is the suffix -*ing*.

John is such a dream*er*. (noun)

This is the suffix -*er*.

If you know a little about suffixes it can help you to spell a word correctly.

Remember . . . | The spelling of a suffix never changes but the spelling of the word to which it is added sometimes does.

Below are some common suffixes and clues to how they are usually used.

-ary	-ly
-ery	-ous
-ory	-ic
-en	-like
-ish	-y
-less	-ful

These suffixes usually make adjectives.

-er	-ship	-ure	-ice
-or	-hood	-ance	-age
-ar	-ness	-ence	-ly
-re	-ism	-ment	

-ing	-ise
-ed	-ize
-ude	-yse
-ure	

These are often verb endings.

These usually form nouns.

Doubling trouble

When you add a suffix beginning with a vowel to a word which ends in one consonant, you sometimes have to *double* the consonant.

The rule is: | With one syllable words you must *double* the *final consonant* when there is only *one* vowel before it.

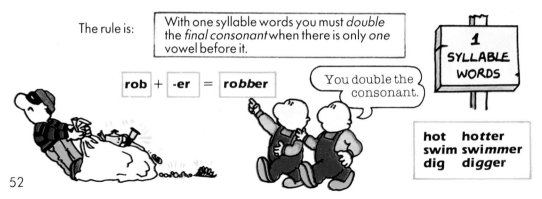

rob + **-er** = **robber**

You double the consonant.

1 SYLLABLE WORDS

hot	hotter
swim	swimmer
dig	digger

If a one syllable word has *two* vowels or ends in *two* consonants you just add the suffix.

No doubling here.

feel	**fee**l**ing**
cool	**cool**ed
wreck	**wre**ck**age**

Doubling in long words

Words with more than one syllable sometimes follow the rule for one syllable words depending on how the word is pronounced.

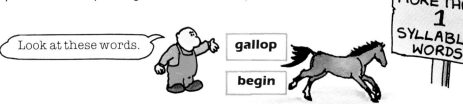

Look at these words.

gallop

begin

MORE THAN 1 SYLLABLE WORDS

They both have two syllables, but they still have *one final consonant* with *one vowel* before it. If you add the suffix -ing to these words *gallop* remains the same — *galloping*, but *begin* doubles the n — *beginning*. The reason for this is that they sound different. When you say "gallop" you stress the first syllable, but when you say "begin" you stress the second syllable.

So the rule is:

> a. If the stress is on the first syllable there is *one consonant* before the suffix.
> b. If the stress is on the second syllable there are *two consonants* before the suffix.

Think which part of the word you stress most.

óffer	**offering**
fásten	**fastened**
propél	**propelling**
forbíd	**forbidden**

Beware "l" ending   Words ending in "l" have a rule of their own.

> Words of more than one syllable which end in *one* "l" after *one* vowel, double the "l" before adding a suffix beginning with a vowel — *no matter where the stress lies.*

Try to remember this.

travel	**travelling**
signal	**signaller**
metal	**metallic**
rebel	**rebellious**

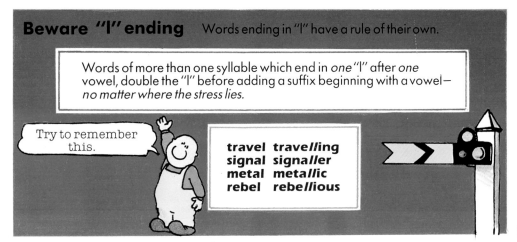

Final "e" words

There are a lot of words which end in a silent "e". (Sometimes this is called a magic "e" or lazy "e".)

A silent "e" is never pronounced, but its presence at the end of a word can change the sound of the other vowel letter in that word from a short sound to a long sound.*

hat + e = hate	
cub + e = cube	
pin + e = pine	

> Adding a silent "e" can change one word into another.

Dropping the "e"

When you add a suffix to a silent "e" word you have to decide whether or not to drop the "e".

Try to remember this rule:

Drop the "e" when the suffix you are adding begins with a vowel.

hope	hoping
forgive	forgiving
love	loving

> Drop the "e" before a vowel.

Note. The letter "y" counts as a vowel when you add it as a suffix.

simple	simply
ease	easy

> This acts as a vowel here.

When do you keep the "e"?

Keep the final "e":

a. When a word ends in *ge* or *ce* before a suffix beginning with *able* or *ous*. You do this to keep the consonant sound soft.

notice	noti*ce*able
courage	coura*ge*ous

b. To prevent confusion.

dye	dyeing
die	dying

c. When the endings *ye, oe* and *ee* come before the suffix.

eye	eyeing
hoe	hoeing
agree	agreeing

What about "ie"?

When a word ends in *ie,* change the "ie" to "y" before adding *-ing.*

die	dying
tie	tying
lie	lying

54

*See page 42.

Final "y" words

If you want to add a suffix to a word which ends in "y" you do have to follow certain rules.

> Consonant here, change to "i".

> If there is a *consonant* before the "y" change the "y" to an "i" and then add the suffix. If there is a *vowel* before the "y", just add the suffix.

marry	**mar*ried***
pity	**pi*tied***
enjoy	**enj*oyed***

> Vowel here, leave the "y".

> But if the suffix begins with "i", keep the "y" because you don't want two "i"s together.

study	**stud*iing*** ✗
study	**stud*ying*** ✓

> Change the "y" to *ie* when you add an *s*.

beauty	**beaut*ies***
apology	**apolog*ies***

Beware

Words that are only *one* syllable *usually* keep the "y", except before *es* and *ed*.

fly	**flyer**
sky	**skywards**
dry	**dryness**
but **dries** **dried**	

Silent "e" quiz

What happens to the "e" when you join these words to the suffixes in brackets?

1. stone(y)
2. declare(ing)
3. excite(ment)
4. love(ing)
5. observe(ant)
6. manage(able)
7. advantage(ous)
8. lone(ly)
9. amaz(ing)
10. inquire(y)
11. hate(ful)
12. stare(ed)

> Use the information on these pages to help you.

What about the "y"?

Can you add the suffix *-ed* to each of the words below remembering what should happen to the "y"?

1. copy
2. deny
3. dry
4. delay
5. ally
6. supply
7. obey
8. cry
9. prophesy
10. dismay
11. apply
12. stay

Double or single "l"?

It is often difficult to know when to write double or single "l", but there are some points to help you.

The *-ful* ending

a. Look at these sentences:

> Emma felt *full of hope* when she started her new job.

> Emma felt *hopeful* when she started her new job.

Notice that:

> When you add *-full* to the end of a word you drop the last "l".

> **hand + full = handful**
> **joy + full = joyful**

There are two words which drop other letters as well.

> **awe + full = awful**
> **skill + full = skilful**

Try to remember these.

b. When the suffix *-ly* is added to a word ending in *-ful* there *will be* a double "l".

> **tearful   tearfully**
> **careful   carefully**

Double or not?

When you want to add the suffix *-ing* or *-ed* to a word ending in "l" you should:

One vowel here.

> Double the "l" if there is *one* vowel before it.

> **pedal   peda*ll*ing**
> **travel   trave*ll*ed**

But don't double the "l" if there are two vowels before it.

> **fail   fai*l*ed**
> **feel   fee*l*ing**

Try these

Fill in the gaps.

Use the suffix *-ful* or *-fully* to complete the sentences?

1. Tom cheer . . . . . took the play . . . . . puppy for a walk.
2. Henrietta tear . . . . . gulped down a huge spoon . . . . . of the aw . . . . . medicine.
3. The bash . . . . . boy waited hope . . . . . for the beauti . . . . . girl to pass by.

Doubling test

Can you join these words and suffixes correctly?

1. patrol(ing)   6. feel(ing)
2. cool(ed)   7. expel(ed)
3. shovel(ing)   8. wheel(ed)
4. marvel(ed)   9. toil(ing)
5. appeal(ing)   10. fulfil(ing)

Tricky endings

It is easy to muddle up the endings of some words because they sound so similar. Some of them just have to be learnt but with others there are some useful tips to help you.

-able   -ible

These are two of the endings most often confused.

1. -able

These two words both make sense as they are.

a. Words ending in *-able* can often be divided into separate words which make sense on their own.

> able + drink = drinkable
> able + adapt = adaptable

b, Words that have "i" before the ending usually take *-able.*

> reliable   enviable   sociable

c. You often use *-able* after a hard "c" or hard "g".

> edu**c**able
> navi**g**able
> ami**c**able

These are hard letters.

d. When you add *-able* to a word that ends in "e", you usually drop the "e".

> love + able = lovable
> value + able = valuable

2. -ible

These words don't make sense on their own.

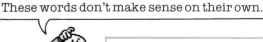

a. Words ending in *-ible cannot* be divided so that the words make sense on their own.

> sens + ible = sensible
> vis + ible = visible

b. Most words with "s" or "ss" before the ending take *-ible.*

> responsible   permissible   possible

c. You often use *-ible* after a soft "c" or soft "g".

> le**g**ible
> eli**g**ible
> invin**c**ible

These are soft letters.

Beware

Can you remember these? Some are quite difficult.

There are some words that don't follow the above rules.

formidable	contemptible
inevitable	resistible
portable	collapsible
memorable	flexible
indomitable	

More tricky endings

-ery -ary

Words ending in -ery are often obvious when spoken.

But there are some tricky -ery words.

People often miss the e sound out when they say these words.

very	bakery
brewery	nursery

cemetery
monastery
stationery

Watch out for these words.

Don't confuse **stationery** (paper, pens, etc.) and **stationary** (not moving). *

If in doubt about which ending to choose use -ary. It is more common.

January	dictionary
February	secretary

-er -or -ar -re -ure

These suffixes often sound similar and it is difficult to know which to choose. There are no rules to follow, but there are some helpful hints.

-or This is usually used when the word means "someone who" or "that which".

A visitor is someone who visits.

-er This occurs most at the end of everyday words.

mother
father
water
brewer
sinner

professor
survivor

-ance -ence -ent -ant

a. You will usually find that the endings -ant and -ent are used for adjectives, while -ance and -ence are noun endings.

An important matter.

The importance of the matter.

A different opinion.

A difference of opinion.

These are adjectives.

These are nouns.

b. Certain consonants tend to be followed by a. The letters "t" and "v" often take -ance.

accept	acceptance
import	importance
relev-	relevance

Try to remember this rule. It may help you.

Every English verb which ends in r preceded by one vowel, and with a stress on the last syllable, forms a noun with -ence.

confér	– conference
refér	– reference
occúr	– occurrence

*See page 44.

-ceed -sede -cede

a. Most words which end in this sound have the suffix -cede.

b. Only one word ends in -sede.

c. Very few words end in -ceed.

precede
recede
concede

Only *one* word ends in -sede.

supersede

succeed   proceed

-ify -efy

Only four words end in -efy. All the rest end in -ify.

stupefy
rarefy
putrefy
liquefy

Only 4.

-ise -ize -yse

Many of these endings come from Old French, Latin or Greek.
If in doubt use the suffix -ise. It is far more common than the other two.

surprise
exercise
disguise

size
prize

analyse
paralyse

-le -el

Most words with this sound end in -le.

battle
nibble
trouble
table

75% end in -le.

but   **unravel**   **travel**
barrel

-ick -ic

Words of two or more syllables end in -ic not -ick.

-ick
(one syllable)
stick
thick
lick
trick
sick

-ic
(two or more syllables)
tonic
comic
static
artistic
fantastic

Fill in the ending

Can you add the right ending to the words below? Use your dictionary when in doubt.

-ary/-ery
1. confection . . .
2. annivers . . .
3. cemet . . .
4. comment . . .
5. fin . . .

-ify/-efy
1. ident . . .
2. stup . . .
3. fort . . .
4. spec . . .
5. liqu . . .

-ent/-ant
1. observ . . .
2. compet . . .
3. defend . . .
4. superintend . . .
5. brilli . . .

59

Other useful rules and tips

Here are some more words which are often mixed up because they sound or look similar.

accept	except	**I *accept* your kind invitation.** **Everyone went to the party *except* Doris.**
diary	dairy	**Tom always wrote everything down in his *diary*.** **The farmer's wife collected milk from the *dairy*.**
quiet	quite	**It was very *quiet* in the country cottage.** **Ben was *quite* good at football.**
legible	eligible	**James wrote the note in capital letters so that it was more *legible*.** **Jane was *eligible* for the job as she had all the right qualifications.**
affect	effect	**The shortage of water will *affect* everyone.** **The medicine did not have any *effect* for a week.**
lightning	lightening	**The thunder roared and the *lightning* flashed.** **She changed the picture she was painting by *lightening* the background.**
principal	principle	**The *principal* of the college had no *principles*.**

One word or two?

These are words which seem to confuse everybody:

Can you make up sentences to show how these words should be used.

Always two	Always one
thank you	today
on to	tomorrow
in front	together
in fact	tonight

Either one or two depending on the meaning

all ways	always
may be	maybe
no body	nobody
any one	anyone
all together	altogether
in to	into
some times	sometimes
every one	everyone

Did you know?

1. The letter "q" is always written as "qu". It never stands by itself.

> *que*en
> *qu*arrel
> re*qu*ire
> in*qu*est

2. No English word ends in the letter "j".

3. No English words ends in the letter "v" except the word spiv.

4. No English word ends in the letter "i" except for taxi (short for taxicab) and some words borrowed from Italian, e.g. macaroni, spaghetti and vermicelli.

Spelling games and puzzles

Crazy spelling

You can have fun taking words you already know how to spell and working out other logical ways of spelling them from the list of vowel sounds on pages 42 and 43, and consonant sounds on page 40.

A good example of this is:

> We had ghuiti on phrighdeigh.*

gh as in cough
ui as in build
ti as in nation

ph as in photo
igh as in high
eigh as in weigh

Try making up crazy spellings for the following words and then show them to your friends to see if they can guess the real spelling:

juice	flesh
cufflink	fluff
siphon	giraffe
coffeebeans	permission
golf	cashew

Computer games

There are now spelling games available to play on your own computer. Some of the most interesting ones are:

1. *Starspell* (BBC Machine, price £6.00)
2. *Witches Brew* (TRS 80 and BBC Machine, price £10.00)
3. *Spelling Builder* (TRS 80, price £12.50)

Dictionaries

Whatever game or puzzle you are playing, you will need to have a dictionary at hand to check your answers. Some useful dictionaries are:

1. *A Basic Dictionary* (Schofield & Sims Ltd)
2. *Oxford Elementary Learner's Dictionary of English* (O.U.P.)
3. *The Concise Oxford Dictionary* (O.U.P.)

*The answer is on page 63.

Palindromes

What do the words below have in common?

madam	minim
level	noon
rotator	radar
deed	civic

They are all *palindromes*. A palindrome is a word, phrase or sentence which reads the same backwards as it does forwards.

Here is a sentence palindrome. Some people think Napoleon could have said it.

> Able was I ere I saw Elba.

Can you think of any more palindromes?

Word crosses and word squares

Look at the cross below. It is made up of two five-letter words which both have the same letter in the middle.

```
        S
        P
  BUILT
        L
        T
```

How many word crosses can you make?

You can also make word squares using four five-letter words.

```
CLEAR
L   A
O   I
T   N
HANDS
```

The word at the top and the word on the left begin with the same letter (C), the last letter of the word on the left (H) gives you the first letter of the bottom word, and so on.

See how many more you can think up. Make up clues to the words and ask your friends if they can answer them.

Answers

What is the real spelling? (page 39)

1. ache
2. behaviour
3. business
4. foreign
5. knowledge
6. precious
7. carriage
8. scissors
9. stomach
10. handkerchief

Try these (page 44)

1. "Come over *here,*" called Fred, but Alice was so busy she didn't *hear.*
2. No-one *knew* the people who had moved into the *new* house.
3. "*No,* I don't *know* the answer to your question.
4. The girl *passed* out as her favourite pop star went *past.*
5. Most people *write* with their *right* hand.
6. Even the *weather* man couldn't tell *whether* it was going to be wet or fine.
7. The silly *witch* forgot *which* spell to use.
8. He told us he *would* be moving to a house on the edge of a *wood.*
9. She didn't know *where* they were going, or what she should *wear.*
10. *Two* of the boys were *too* young *to* go *to* the football match.

Spot the mistakes (page 45)

1. Cynthia had such a *pain* in her *heel* it *made* her *groan.*
2. Fred was so greedy he ate a *whole currant* cake without offering anyone else a *piece.*
3. Tom had such huge *muscles* he could lift *two* cars with his *bare* hands.
4. The drunkard spent the night in a prison *cell* and was *fined* for using *foul* language.

Test yourself (page 46)

1. addresses
2. gardens
3. cases
4. losses
5. wishes
6. marches
7. lashes
8. princesses
9. pitches
10. dishes
11. ships
12. crashes
13. taxes
14. tables
15. arches
16. houses
17. torches
18. splashes

Add the right ending (page 47)

1. toys
2. miseries
3. donkeys
4. deputies
5. countries
6. quays
7. memories
8. jellies
9. trays
10. robberies

Which of these pairs are wrong? (page 48)

4. calf calves
6. knife knives
7. leaf leaves
13. shelf shelves
15. elf elves
19. gulf gulfs
21. loaf loaves
22. belief beliefs

Puzzle it out (page 49)
Plural endings:

1. antennae
2. cargoes
3. axes
4. salmon
5. mottos or mottoes
6. brothers-in-law
7. women
8. buffaloes
9. geese
10. pianos
11. tomatoes
12. men-of-war

Puzzle it out (page 49) Singular endings:

1. leaf
2. holiday
3. radish
4. patch
5. echo
6. kangaroo
7. court-martial
8. opportunity
9. city
10. hippopotamus
11. abscess
12. oasis

Spot the mistakes (page 49)

1. Kenne*dys*
2. pupp*ies*
3. lorr*ies*
4. bus*es*
5. leav*es*
6. roo*fs*
7. butterfl*ies*
8. pupp*ies*
9. donk*eys*
10. bush*es*
11. lunch*es*
12. tomat*oes*
13. mosquit*oes*

Test 1 (page 50) Add the right prefixes

*de*part	*mis*take	*ante*natal
*dis*agreement	*mis*understanding	*anti*septic
*de*lay	*dis*please	*anti*climax
*dis*obedient	*dis*satisfied	*ante*chamber
*il*legal	*in*discreet	*pro*ceed
*im*moral	*un*reliable	*pre*pare
*il*logical	*in*expensive	*pre*caution
*im*possible	*un*important	*pro*vide

Test 2 (page 51)

*ad*vance – towards	*sub*merge – under
*de*scend – down	*mal*formation – bad
*super*vise – above (over)	*en*trance – in
*bi*lingual – two	*ex*it – out

Test 3 (page 51)

*un*employment	*dis*appear
*mis*fortune	*ir*responsible
*dis*respectful	*non*alcoholic
*un*pleasant	*im*patient

Silent "e" quiz (page 55)

1. stony
2. declaring
3. excitement
4. loving
5. observant
6. manageable
7. advantageous
8. lonely
9. amazing
10. inquiry
11. hateful
12. stared

What about the "y"? (page 55)

1. copied
2. denied
3. dried
4. delayed
5. allied
6. supplied
7. obeyed
8. cried
9. prophesied
10. dismayed
11. applied
12. stayed

Try these (page 56)

1. cheerfully, playful.
2. tearfully, spoonful, awful.
3. bashful, hopefully, beautiful.

Doubling test (page 56)

1. patrolling
2. cooled
3. shovelling
4. marvelled
5. appealing
6. feeling
7. expelled
8. wheeled
9. toiling
10. fulfilled

Fill in the ending (page 59)

1. confectionery
2. anniversary
3. cemetery
4. commentary
5. finery
6. identify
7. stupefy
8. fortify
9. specify
10. liquefy
11. observant
12. competent
13. defendant
14. superintendent
15. brilliant

Crazy spelling (page 61)

We had fish on Friday.

63

Index/glossary

abbreviation, 36 The shortened form of a word using some of the letters or just the initials: e.g. Feb. – February, C. A. Wilson.

adjective, 36, 52, 58 Describing word which gives a fuller meaning to a noun: e.g. *pretty* girl, *vicious* dog.

adverb, 36 Word which "modifies" or tells you more information about a verb. Usually answers the questions. How? When? Where? or Why? in connection with the verb.

apostrophe, 44 Punctuation mark which shows: (1) that one or more letters have been missed out: e.g. didn't; (2) possession.

conjunction, 36 Word used to connect clauses or sentences; or to connect words within a clause, e.g. and, but, or.

consonant, 35, 36, 38, 39, 40, 42, 47, 52, 53, 55, 58, 61 Any letter of the alphabet that is not a vowel (a e i o u). [When combined with a vowel forms a syllable.]

etymology, 34 Study of how words are formed and where they come from.

homophone, 44, 45 A word which sounds the same as another word but is spelt differently.

hyphen, 37, 48 Punctuation mark used to link two or more words together to make one word or expression.

negative prefix, 50 A prefix which, when added to the front of a word, gives it the opposite meaning: e.g. possible – impossible (see prefix).

noun 36, 45, 58 Word used as the name of a person, thing or place: e.g. dog, man.

palindrome, 61 Word, phrase or sentence which reads the same backwards as it does forwards: e.g. level.

phonetics, 39 System of spelling words by representing sounds by symbols.

prefix, 36, 50 Small addition to a word made by joining on one or more letters at the beginning: e.g. ex, pre, anti.

plural, 46, 47, 48, 49 A plural word refers to more than one thing: e.g. books, women, lilies.

pronunciation, 38, 39 The way you say words.

"received pronunciation", 39 The standard pronunciation "without any accent" used in this book and most dictionaries.

silent letters, 37, 38, 41 Letters which are present in a word, but are not sounded when the word is pronounced: e.g. knife.

singular, 46 The name referring to one thing or group of things: e.g. man, book, flock.

suffix, 36, 52, 53, 54, 55, 56 A letter or group of letters added to the end of a word to change the way you use it: e.g. coward*ly*

syllable, 35, 38, 39, 53, 55, 58 A combination of one or more vowels and consonants which can make one short word, or part of a longer word: e.g. cat, won-der-ful.

verb, 36, 45, 58 Word which shows some kind of action or being: e.g. run, jump, think, is, was, were.

vowel, 35, 37, 38, 39, 42, 47, 52, 53, 54, 55, 56, 58, 61 There are five vowels in the alphabet – a e i o u. All the rest are consonants.

The definition *reindeer* is reproduced from the *Concise Oxford Dictionary* (7th edition 1982) with kind permission of Oxford University Press.

ENGLISH GRAMMAR

Consultant: Diccon Swan

English Grammar: Contents

With thanks to Peter Traskey of Milton Abbey School, Dorset.

What is grammar?

Grammar is a set of rules and guidelines to help you use language correctly. If you want to learn a trade or skill you have to know how to handle the tools of the trade. If you want to express yourself well you have to know how to handle the tools of language.

Why should we have rules?

Rules always seem boring, dull and pointless, and breaking rules is fun. But imagine you were playing a game of cricket. Like all games it is based on a set of rules. If some of the players in the team decided to break the rules and do what they wanted, the game would become chaotic. You would not know what was happening and everyone would become confused.

This can also happen with language. If you do not follow the guidelines it will lose its meaning and people will not understand what you are trying to communicate.

How can grammar help?

Most of us ignore grammar in our everyday speech and in writing quick messages. It is, however, important to be accurate, clear and formal in certain aspects of life:

1. Jobs

Nowadays it is difficult to find a job. No matter how talented or well-qualified you are at something, there always seem to be hundreds of other people just as suitable.

If you apply for a job sending a letter which is full of grammatical mistakes, the employer will give preference to someone with the same qualifications who has expressed himself correctly.

2. Other kinds of letters and communications

Sometimes you may want to write or speak to someone in authority. It could be to explain a situation, complain about something or even to make someone see your point of view.

It's like this officer ...

If you can express yourself clearly and concisely the point you are making will be easily understood. If, however, you write or speak in a rambling, unintelligible way which does not convey your point of view, people may take advantage of you or misinterpret what you say.

3. Creative writing

There are times when you may want to write something creative, like a poem, a story, or even just your thoughts. Many people feel that in this case it is not important to write correctly as it prevents you from writing spontaneously. This can be true. If, however, you want to add style and variety to this kind of expression, and to convey it effectively to others, it will help if you have some knowledge of how the English language works.

What shall I write today?

Most famous writers, artists and musicians have based their creative talents on some kind of rules.

Parts of speech

What we say is called speech. Speech is rather like a train. It can be in one long burst, or it can be lots of short ones (little trains going in different directions).

Like a train it is made up of carriages or trucks which by themselves do not do very much, but, when linked together to form the train, they are very useful.

The trucks are like the words in speech — they can be individual things but they need others to make them into a useful whole.

The whole train is like a sentence — a group of words that makes sense and gets us somewhere. Trains also have to keep on the lines in order to get anywhere, and the track is like grammar; it lays down the direction and makes sure the train gets somewhere.

In this book you will find all the different parts of speech you can use, and how to join them into different kinds of sentences. You will also find tips on how to avoid common mistakes in English, and hints on how to write English clearly and with style.

As you read you may well come across words you have never met before. If so, try looking in the index/glossary where there is an explanation of some of the harder words.

> Grammar will keep you on the right lines.

The parts of speech — brief guide

There are eight different parts of speech:

1. Noun

Word used for naming a person, animal, place or thing (e.g. William, mouse, shop, ladder).

2. Pronoun

Word used to refer to a person or thing without giving a name. Takes the place of a noun (e.g. he, she, them, him).

4. Adjective

Word used to describe a *noun* or *pronoun* (e.g. fat, dangerous, new, wooden).

4. Verb

Often called a "doing" word. Word used to describe action or existence (e.g. run, was, kicked, are).

5. Adverb

Word used generally to modify (tell you more about) a *verb*, but can tell you more about any word other than a noun or pronoun (e.g. quickly, soon, very, rather).

6. Preposition

Word used for showing what one person or thing has to do with another person or thing — usually where they are in relation to one another (e.g. with, under, on).

7. Conjunction

Word used to join words and clauses (e.g. and, but, when).

8. Interjection (or Exclamation)

Word used to express exclamation (e.g. Oh! Hello).

Nouns

A noun is a word used for naming a person, an animal, a place or a thing.

These words are all nouns.

| bird | ladder | windowcleaner | shop |

To decide whether a word is a noun, ask yourself, "Does it tell me something's name?" If the answer is, "Yes", the word is a noun.

under ✗

table ✓

Does it tell me the name of something?

Nouns can usually have "the", or "a", or "an" in front of them. Try putting "the" in front of the words on the right to find out which of them are nouns.

saucepan heat
finger daffodil
happy never
rocket sky
sometime have

Can I say "the never"?

Names of particular people are nouns, even though you can't put "the" in front of them.

Alice Albert Ethel

Spot the nouns

Can you pick out the nouns in the list of words below?

ugly	under
box	slowly
David	in
wonderful	cup
dog	when
bottle	silly

How many nouns can you find in the sentences below?

1. Boris, the cat, ran across the road.
2. Cynthia was wearing a beautiful red dress.
3. Tom had a dog, a hamster, a white rabbit and a budgerigar.
4. Mary has sold her old car in favour of a new bicycle.
5. The poor old man had only a bed, a table and one chair.

Singular or plural

Nouns can be either singular (referring to one single person or thing):

| bat | box | berry |

Is this singular or plural?

It is singular.

or plural:

| bats | boxes | berries |

leaf

Four kinds of nouns

There are four different kinds of nouns.
These are: 1. *proper* nouns, 2. *common* nouns, 3. *collective* nouns, 4. *abstract* nouns.

1. *A proper noun* is a noun that refers to a particular person or thing, rather than a general class of thing.

Samson
Mexico
Monday
August
Gulliver's Travels

> Proper nouns have capital letters.

> You can't usually put "the" or "a" with proper nouns.

2. *A common noun* names a kind of person or thing. It is called "common" because the name is common to all persons or things of the same kind.

man
country
day
month
book

> Compare these words with the proper nouns shown above.

3. *A collective noun* describes a group or collection of people or things.

These words are all collective nouns.

army (a collection of soldiers)
bunch (a collection of flowers)
team (a collection of players)
pack (a collection of hounds)
swarm (a collection of bees)

> Some collective nouns describe a definite number of something. "Pair" and "dozen" are both collective nouns.

4. *Abstract nouns* describe things that cannot actually be seen, heard, smelt, felt or tasted.

sleep
honesty
boredom
freedom
power

Gender

A noun is either masculine, feminine, common or neuter in gender.

| actor | actress | teacher | book |

> Common (either masculine or feminine)

> Neuter (neither masculine nor feminine)

Masculine   Feminine

Pronouns

Sometimes you refer to a person or thing not by its actual name, but by another word which stands for it. The word you use to stand for a noun is called a pronoun (which means "for a noun").

**Jack plays his oboe every evening.
He is learning very fast.**

"He" is a pronoun. In this sentence it stands for Jack.

To decide if a word is a pronoun ask yourself, "Does it stand for a noun?"

You use pronouns so that you do not have to repeat the same nouns over again. They make speaking and writing much quicker and clearer. Compare the two sentences below.

When Barnaby stroked the cat and listened to it purring softly, he felt calm and peaceful.

If there were no pronouns you would have to say this.

When Barnaby stroked the cat and listened to the cat purring softly, Barnaby felt calm and peaceful.

Pronoun

The words in the boxes below are all pronouns. They can all stand instead of the name of a person, place or thing.

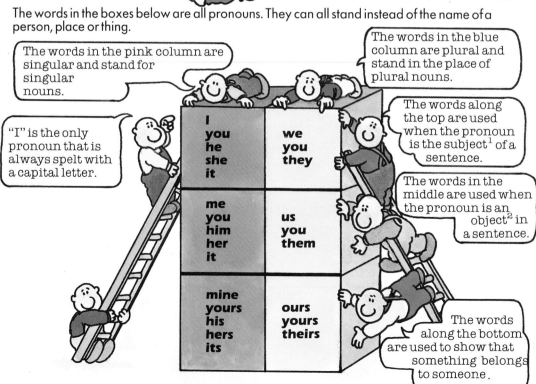

The words in the pink column are singular and stand for singular nouns.

The words in the blue column are plural and stand in the place of plural nouns.

"I" is the only pronoun that is always spelt with a capital letter.

The words along the top are used when the pronoun is the subject[1] of a sentence.

The words in the middle are used when the pronoun is an object[2] in a sentence.

The words along the bottom are used to show that something belongs to someone.

I you he she it	we you they
me you him her it	us you them
mine yours his hers its	ours yours theirs

[1] & [2]. To find out about subjects and objects in a sentence see page 74

Problems with "I" and "me"

In some sentences it is difficult to decide whether to use "me" or "I".

Would you say this?

Or this?

Carol and me are going on holiday.

Carol and I are going on holiday.

Whenever you find it difficult to decide, try splitting the sentence into two short sentences, like this:

Carol is going on holiday.

You could not say this, could you?

I am going on holiday.

Me am going on holiday.

✓ Carol and I are going on holiday.

This sentence was the correct one.

After prepositions* you always use the object form of the pronoun.

Would you say this?

It is a secret between Jo and I.

or this?

It is a secret between Jo and me.

"between" is a preposition.

This one is right.

Find the pronouns

Can you find the pronouns in these sentences?

1. She went out to find them.
2. We asked him if he was feeling better.
3. "I think this is yours," she said.
4. You should ask her if she wants to join us.
5. It isn't yours, it's mine!
6. They took me home with them.

Other types of pronoun

The pronouns shown in the chart on the opposite page are called personal pronouns and are probably used more than any others. But there are several other types of pronoun. Here is a list of some of the different types:

1. **Personal pronouns** (I, you, etc.).

2. **Reflexive pronouns** (myself, yourself, himself, herself, itself, ourselves, themselves). These are called reflexive because they *reflect* back to an earlier noun or pronoun.

3. **Relative pronouns** (who, whom, whose, which, that, what). These pronouns help to connect or *relate* one part of a sentence to another.

4. **Interrogative pronouns** (who, whose, whom, which, what). These pronouns help to ask questions or *interrogate.*

5. **Demonstrative pronouns** (this, that, these, those). These point out a person or thing specifically.

6. **Indefinite pronouns** (words like any, each, several, some, and many more). These refer to people or things generally rather than specifically.

*See pages 82 and 83

Adjectives

An adjective is a word which "qualifies" (tells you more about) a noun or pronoun. It answers the question, "What is it like?".

This tells you about the jacket.

The burglar was wearing a *black* jacket, a *furry* hat and a *large* mask over his face.

This tells you more about the hat.

This word tells you more about the mask.

An adjective usually comes before a noun but sometimes it can be separated from its noun and come afterwards.

Ben looked *frightened*.

The traffic warden in our area is very *fierce*.

Different types of adjectives

1. *"Asking" adjectives (interrogative)*

Which hat do you prefer?

"What" is another asking adjective.

2. *Possessive adjectives* — these show ownership.

Sue never brushes *her* hair.

This shows you *whose* hair it is.

Other possessive adjectives are:

my	our	their	his	your

3. *Adjectives of number or quantity* — these deal with the *amount* of something.

All numbers are adjectives.

She invited *five* friends for breakfast.

She did not have *any* food left.

Here are some adjectives of quantity:

much more most little less least no some any enough sufficient all whole half quarter

4. *"Pointing-out" adjectives (demonstrative)*

These are singular.

That man stole *this* handbag.

Those apples and *these* pears are bad.

These are plural.

72

Comparing things

1. There are three forms of any adjective that you can use when you describe a noun or pronoun. Look at the sentences below:

She is *tall*.

The word *tall* is an ordinary adjective.

> You use a comparative adjective when you are *comparing* two people or things.

She is *taller* than her sister.

The word *taller* is a comparative adjective.

She is the *tallest* in her family.

The word *tallest* is a superlative adjective.

> You use a superlative when referring to at least three people or things.

The comparative adjective is made by adding -*er* to the adjective, and the superlative is made by adding -*est* to the adjective and putting *the* in front of it.

2. Some adjectives have to change their spelling slightly to form their comparatives and superlatives.

a. If the adjective ends in an "e", you just add -*r* for the comparative and -*st* for the superlative.

larg*e*   larg*er*   larg*est*

b. If the adjective ends in "y", this letter is changed to "i" before adding -*er* and -*est*.

pretty   prett*ier*   prett*iest*

> "y" changes to "i".

c. Some adjectives double their final letter before adding -*er* and -*est*.

thin   thi*nn*er   thi*nn*est

3. Where adding -*er* and *est* would make an adjective sound awkward, you form the comparative and superlative by putting *more* and *the most* in front of it.

She is beautiful.

She is *more* beautiful.

She is *the most* beautiful.

> Longer words often sound awkward if you add -*er* or -*est* to them.

4. Some of the most common adjectives form their comparatives and superlatives in an odd or "irregular" way that does not follow the normal rules.

Adjective	Comparative	Superlative
good	better	best
bad	worse	worst
little	less	least
much	more	most
many	more	most

Verbs

A verb is a word, or a group of words, that tells you what a person or thing is being or doing. It is often called a *doing word*: e.g. running, eating, sitting.

A verb is the most important word in a sentence; without it a sentence does not make any sense.

He *drank* his tea.	He his tea.
She *went* to the shops.	She to the shops.

These don't make sense at all.

All sentences have a *subject* and a *verb*. The subject is the person or thing doing the action.

Cats purr.	*The wind* blows.	*Birds* fly.

Some sentences can be just the subject and the verb, but in some sentences the verb has to have an *object* as well.

Cats chase *mice.*	Alice liked *Ben.*	King Alfred burnt *the cakes.*

The object tells you "what" or "whom" the verb affects.

King Alfred burnt what?
King Alfred burnt *the cakes.*

Think of all the actions you can do. These are all verbs.

Transitive and intransitive verbs

When a verb takes the action from the subject across to the object it is called a *transitive* verb.

Squirrels collect nuts.

Here the squirrel is doing the action to the nuts.

Tom polished his shoes.

The verbs that don't have any objects are called *intransitive* verbs.

Your socks smell.

The boat sank.

The telephone rang.

Intransitive verbs make sense on their own they do not need an object.

Some verbs can be both transitive and intransitive.

He smells.	She is playing.
He smelt the burning toast.	She is playing the piano.

74

The infinitive

The infinitive is *the name* of the verb, e.g. go, catch, run, sleep. It usually has "to" in front of it, but you can use it without.

to wish

> **She began *to wish* she had never set out.**

to go

> **Bill did not know where *to go*.**

(to) work

> **Our teacher makes us *work* hard.**

This would sound odd with "to" in front of it.

Tenses

The word "tense" comes from the Latin word "tempus" — meaning time. The tense of the verb tells you the time at which the action takes place.

There are three main tenses:

Present — I eat.

Past — I ate.

Future — I shall eat.

Look at the chart below. It will help you sort out how the verbs and tenses work. The verb "to stay" is used as an example.

Subject	Present	Past	Future
I	stay (am staying)	stayed (was staying)	shall stay (shall be staying)
you (singular)	stay (are staying)	stayed (were staying)	will stay (will be staying)
he/she/it	stays (is staying)	stayed (was staying)	will stay (will be staying)
we	stay (are staying)	stayed (were staying)	shall stay (shall be staying)
you (plural)	stay (are staying)	stayed (were staying)	will stay (will be staying)
they	stay (are staying)	stayed (were staying)	will stay (will be staying)

The verbs in brackets are another version of the verb above them. This is called the *continuous* tense because it shows that the action is going on for some time.

Auxiliary (helping) verbs

to be **to have**

A verb is often made up of more than one word:

| **He is talking.** | **They have worked.** | **We shall be running.** |

The actual verb-word is helped out by parts of the special verbs: the verb *to be* and the verb *to have*. These helping verbs are called *auxiliary* verbs. They help to form the tenses.

I *was* eating.

I *have* slept.

shall **will**

1 *Shall* and *will* are also parts of verbs. They help to make the future tense. *Shall* is used with *I* and *we*; all the other pronouns * use *will*.

| **I *shall* return.** | **You *will* be late.** |

2 You can use *shall* and *will* to show a command, a promise or an expression of determination. In order to do this you change the rule around.

instead of: **I shall go out.**

you use: **I *will* go out.**

Instead of: **He will get up soon.**

You do this to stress the point you are making.

you use: **He *shall* get up soon.**

Spot the verb

Can you spot the verbs below?:

1. Diana cleaned the floor.
2. The dog is barking.
3. Dad has made the tea.
4. Jo will be watching the match.
5. Mum has crashed the car.
6. The chef is tossing a pancake.

Fill in the missing verb

Can you fill in the missing verb?

1. We . . . . going on holiday soon.
2. The baby . . . . been crying all day.
3. They . . . . be late if they don't hurry.
4. I . . . . miss you when you go.
5. I . . . . *not* do as you say!
6. Tom . . . . mending the fuse.
7. They . . . . working for hours.

* For more about pronouns see pages 70 and 71

Active and passive

You can use verbs in two different ways.
These are often called "voices".

1. The active "voice"

Look at this sentence.

> **Tom *kicked* the ball.**

Here Tom (subject) is doing the action of kicking. *Kicked* is an *active* verb.

2. The passive "voice"

You can say the above sentence the other way round.

> **The ball *was kicked* by Tom.**

Here the ball (subject) is having the action done to it. *Was kicked* is a *passive* verb.

The active "voice" is stronger and more direct than the passive "voice". The active is used much more often because it is usually shorter and easier to read.

Active	Passive
James *caught* ten fish.	**Ten fish *were caught* by James.**
Mum *baked* five cakes.	**Five cakes *were baked* by Mum.**

These are much easier.

If you use the passive voice it can give a different kind of emphasis to your sentences. For example, when you see public notices they are often written in the passive because it is less aggressive and abrupt than the active.

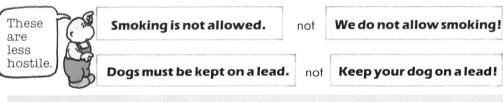

These are less hostile.

Smoking is not allowed. not **We do not allow smoking!**

Dogs must be kept on a lead. not **Keep your dog on a lead!**

Change around

Can you change these sentences so that the verbs are in the *passive* voice?

1. The cat ate a huge, black spider.
2. Doris cleans the silver every fortnight.
3. Mum mowed the lawn early this morning.
4. The burglars hid the money under the bed.
5. Jo threw the rubbish into the dustbin.
6. The groom brushed the horse.
7. The gardener waters the plants.
8. He ordered a taxi to take her home.

Participles

Participles are parts of a verb. They are called participles because they "participate", or take part, in forming the verb. They usually follow the auxiliary verbs "to be" and "to have".[1]

Participles help to form the tenses of verbs, but they can also act as other parts of speech as well. There are two kinds of participle: past and present.

Past participle

The past participle helps to make the past tense of a verb. It usually follows "has", "have", "had" or "was".

The past participle usually ends in *-ed, -d, -t, -en* or *-n*.

| Kim was ***bitten*** by a mosquito. |

| Tom had ***fallen*** out of bed. |

| Harriet has ***walked*** home. |

heard learnt chosen moved

dug bought begun gone

But here are some examples of irregular endings.

The past participle as an adjective

The past participle can be used as an adjective as well as a verb.

These are verbs.

| Jane wore a ***creased*** dress. |

| Jane's dress was ***creased***. |

| Jim could not write with his ***broken*** pencil. |

| Jim's pencil had ***broken***. |

These are adjectives.

Can you see which nouns the adjectives are describing?

Present participle

The present participle is the part of the verb which ends in *-ing*.

| The baby is ***crying***. |

Although it is called the *present* participle it is used to form *all* tenses with the help of the auxiliary verbs, "to have" and "to be".

| Doris has been ***cleaning*** the house all day. |

| Graham is ***working***. |

| We will be ***going*** tomorrow. |

Verbs using the present participle are said to be in the continuous tense[2] whether past, present or future.

[1]See page 76   [2]See page 75

The present participle as an adjective

In the sentences below the present participle is used as an adjective.

> **She painted a picture of the *rising* sun.**

> **She could not sleep for the noise of *chirping* birds, *braying* donkeys, *howling* dogs and *whining* mosquitoes.**

> Can you think of any more participles that can be used in this way?

Beware   It is very easy to get confused when using the present participle as an adjective or in adjectival phrases. People often use it wrongly.

Look at this sentence:

✗
> **Driving along the road, a cow appeared in front of me.**

This means a cow was driving along the road.

When the participle is acting as an adjective it qualifies a noun or pronoun like any other adjective. In the sentence above the adjectival participle is qualifying "cow" which creates the wrong impression.

If you are not sure whether you have used a participle correctly, try to re-phrase the sentence to avoid the problem.

> **As I was driving along the road, a cow appeared in front of me.**   ✓

The present participle as a noun (gerund)

The present participle can be used as a noun. When it is used in this way it is called a *gerund*.

> **Edward did not approve of the *hunting* of animals and the *shooting* of birds.**

> **The *giggling* of the girls annoyed the boys.**

> Notice that you can put "the" in front of it like any other noun.

A gerund acts just like any other noun, therefore it can be described by an adjective.

> **The *awful wailing* of tom-cats went on all night.**

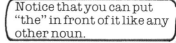

> **The *vicious killing* of the old man shocked everyone.**

Beware
You always use a possessive *adjective* instead of a pronoun with a gerund.

> **People regretted *his* going.**   ✓
> not   **People regretted him going.**   ✗

> Remember.

> **I don't like *your* being here.**   ✓
> not   **I don't like you being here.**   ✗

Adverbs

An adverb modifies (makes more precise) any word in a sentence other than a noun or a pronoun. Usually it tells you more about the verb.

An adverb nearly always answers the questions How? When? Where? or Why?

Look at this sentence:

> **Ben returned.**

It makes complete sense on its own, but you don't know how, when, where or why Ben returned. You can say more about Ben's return by using adverbs, or adverbial phrases.[1]

> **Ben returned *home* (where) *quickly* (how), *yesterday* (when), *to watch the match* (why).**

Adverbs can be one word or a group of words. When there is a group of words not containing a verb, it is a *phrase.* If the group of words contains a verb but does not make complete sense on its own, it is a *clause.*[2]

Adverbs of degree

All the adverbs above modify the verb "returned". But adverbs can also modify adjectives and other adverbs. These are sometimes called *adverbs of degree*. All adverbs of degree answer the question *How?*

> Here the adverb tells you more about the adjective.

> **It was *too* hot to play tennis.**

> **Mum looked *very* different with her new hairstyle.**

> **Tom got up *remarkably* early this morning.**

> **He painted the garden wall *rather* carelessly.**

> Here the adverb modifies *another* adverb.

Forming adverbs

Most adverbs in English end in *-ly* and come from adjectives.

soft	**– softly**
right	**– rightly**

Note! If the adjective ends in *-y*, e.g. pretty, you change the "y" into "i" before adding the *-ly*.

busy	**– busily**
weary	**– wearily**

Beware

Don't confuse adverbs with *adjectives* that end in *-ly*.

> These are adjectives.

> **prickly, manly, friendly**

If you want to make an adverb out of adjectives like these, you turn them into adverbial phrases.

> **He chatted friendlily.** ✗

> You can't do this.

> **He chatted *in a friendly way*.** ✓

80

Sentence adverbs

Adverbs can appear in a sentence on their own. They can change the whole meaning of that sentence. These are called *sentence adverbs*.

Here are some sentence adverbs.

neverless still moreover

however on the other hand

> She felt, *however,* that he was not entirely honest.

> He was, *nevertheless,* a loyal friend.

Placing the adverb

Make sure that you place adverbs in the sentence correctly, otherwise the meaning of the sentence may change or become confused.

These *common adverbs* are often put in the wrong place.

only just almost even mainly also

These should be placed immediately *before* the word they modify.

Look at this sentence:

> Pat gave Polly a pound.

ONLY

Try inserting "only" in every possible position in the sentence. How many different meanings can you make?

Adverb or adjective?

Some words can be either adverbs or adjectives depending on what they do in a sentence, e.g. fast, hard, late.

If they answer the questions How? When? Where? or Why? they are adverbs: but if they answer the question "What is it like?" they are adjectives, and will be telling you more about a specific noun.

> LIfe is *hard.* (adjective)

> Kim works *hard.* (adverb)

> The train arrived *early.* (adverb)

> I took an *early* train. (adjective)

Can you think of any more adverbs that can be used as adjectives?

Worn-out adverbs

Nowadays people tend to use certain adverbs of degree to stress what they are saying, when in fact they add little or nothing at all to the meaning of the sentence.

This letter will give you an idea of what to avoid.

> Dear Sarah,
> Thank you <u>awfully</u> for your note.
> I had an <u>absolutely</u> fabulous holiday, got <u>terribly</u> brown and met some <u>incredibly</u> interesting people.
> We went to some <u>frightfully</u> expensive restaurants and had some <u>superbly</u> delicious meals!
> We must meet soon,
> love
> Claude.

The adverbs underlined do not add much to the meaning of the sentence and lessen the effect of the adjectives.

Prepositions

Prepositions are words which show the relationship of one thing to another. They often tell you *where* one thing is in relation to another, or the "position" that it is in. They are always attached to a noun or pronoun.

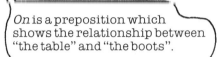

> **The boots are *on* the table.**

Where are the boots? = *On* the table.

> **Fred goes running *before* breakfast.**

On is a preposition which shows the relationship between "the table" and "the boots".

Here are some more examples of prepositions:

across the road

over the fence

into the garden

past the dustbins

under a tree

up the stairs

in the bath

down the bannisters

Preposition or adverb?

Words that are prepositions can also do the work of adverbs. It is often difficult to sort out which is which. The best way to decide is to remember that a preposition is *always* followed by a noun or a pronoun.

> **The cat climbed *up* the tree.**

Up is a *preposition* which tells you the relationship between "the cat" and "the tree".

> **The cat climbed *up*.**

Up is an *adverb* which tells you *where* the cat climbed.

Here are some of the prepositions which can be used as adverbs:

in	on	before	behind	near
below	along	through	down	over	under

Prepositions and pronouns

If a preposition is followed by a pronoun the pronoun is always in its *object form*.[1]

✓ | **She sat near *me*.**

She sat near *I*. ✗

✓ | **He gave it to *her*.**

He gave it to *she*. ✗

Sometimes a preposition is followed by two words linked by *and*.

Look at these sentences:

A strange thing happened to *me*.

A strange thing happened to *David* and *me*.

A strange thing happened to David and *I*. ✗

If you changed the noun David to a pronoun, *both* pronouns would be in the object form.

A strange thing happened to *him* and *me*.

Who and whom?

The pronoun[2] *who* changes to *whom* after a preposition.

They are the people *to whom* I spoke.

He is someone *for whom* I have great respect.

Prepositions often confused

in/into

In is used to indicate a position.

The children are *in* bed.

He is *in* the swimming pool.

Into is used with a verb of motion to show entrance.

The children climbed *into* bed.

He fell *into* the swimming pool.

to/till/until

a. The word *to* can be used for place *and* time; *till* and *until* can be used for time only.

or | **We work from 8.00 a.m. *to* 6.00 p.m.**
We work from 8.00 a.m. *till* 6.00 p.m.

If there is no *from*, you use *till* or *until* instead of *to*.

We worked *until* dawn.

b. The word *to* is used for place.

He drove *to* the crossroads.

You can't write: ✗

He drove *until* the crossroads.

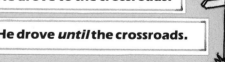

[1] See pages 70-71   [2] See page 71

Connecting words (Conjunctions)

Words used to connect other words are called conjunctions. They join together words, phrases, clauses and sentences. Below you can see four conjunctions, each joining two words together.

| **Bill *and* Ben** |

| **sad *but* true** |

> Conjunctions are connecting words.

| **young *yet* wise** |

| **friends *or* enemies** |

Conjunctions are important for linking sentences together. Without them speech and writing would sound very jerky.

Look at these sentences:

| **Jim turned round.** | **Jim bumped into the fat lady.** |

| **Jim turned round *and* bumped into the fat lady.** |

> Jim is the subject of both sentences so you can leave out the second Jim when you join the two sentences together

Conjunction pairs

Conjunctions often appear in pairs.

| **He likes *both* jam *and* honey.** |

| **Cedric owns *not only* a house *but also* a castle.** |

| **Joanne is *neither* good *nor* clever.** |

| **They cannot decide *whether* to stay *or* go.** |

Beware   When you use these pairs of conjunctions you have to make sure you put the conjunctions *before* the words they join.

| **Rod *not only* played the guitar *but also* the drums.** |

| **Rod played *not only* the guitar *but also* the drums.** |

| **She *neither* was at home *nor* at work.** | **She was *neither* at home *nor* at work.** |

Different kinds of conjunctions

1. Certain conjunctions are used to join two sentences of equal importance. These are called *co-ordinating* conjunctions.

> and but for or yet however
> as well as so nor both therefore

Simon likes coffee.	Anna likes tea.

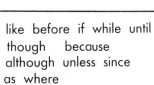

> These two sentences are just as important as each other.

Simon likes coffee, *but* Anna likes tea.

She went to the shops.	She bought a box of chocolates.

She went to the shop *and* bought a box of chocolates.

2. Sometimes you join two sentences together so that one of them contains a major statement (main clause)★, and the other contains a minor statement (the subordinate clause)★. The conjunctions used to do this are called *subordinating* conjunctions.

> These are the main statements.

He was angry *because* I was late.

> like before if while until
> though   because
> although unless since
> as   where
> whenever   wherever

Emma cleaned her teeth *before* she went to bed.

3. When you want to join two contrasting statements you can use particular conjunctions which add weight to the point you are making.

> though although however but
> nevertheless

Kim was very tired, *nevertheless* she worked all weekend.

She did not stop to rest *although* she felt ill.

What is missing?

Can you fill in the missing conjunctions in the sentences below?

1. Henry got up late . . . . he was on holiday.
2. He wanted to have a bath . . . . the water was cold.
3. He did not know . . . . to wear his jeans . . . . his shorts.
4. He ate a plateful of bacon . . . . eggs, ... drinking five cups of tea.

Which pair?

Can you put the correct pair of conjunctions into these sentences?

1. Celia could not decide . . . . it was true . . . . not.
2. They owned . . . . . a Mercedes . . . . a Range Rover.
3. This child is . . . . laughing . . . . crying.
4. Alice is . . . . tall . . . . short; she is average height.
5. Sam has . . . . a car . . . . a motorbike.

★See page 89

Sentences

A sentence is a group of words which makes complete sense on its own.

A sentence has two parts — the person or thing which the sentence is about, called *the subject*; and what is written or said about the subject, called *the predicate*.

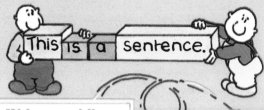

This is a sentence.

Look at this sentence:

James fell off his motorbike.

James is the subject of the sentence; the rest of the sentence is the predicate.

The predicate always includes the verb of the sentence.

***fell** off his motorbike.*

This is the verb.

Sometimes the subject can be a group of words:

James, tired and weary from so much work, fell off his motorbike.

Who fell? "James, tired and weary from so much work," fell and is the *subject*.

The subject of the sentence is not always found at the beginning, it can also be in the middle or at the end. If it were always in the same place what we say and write would sound very boring.

The aeroplane flew over the mountains.

Over the mountains *the aeroplane* flew.

Over the mountains flew *the aeroplane*.

Sentences with a purpose

The sentences above are straightforward statements, but sentences can have different purposes:

1. **Statements** — sentences which state facts.

    It is very hot.

2. **Questions** — sentences which ask for an answer.

    Are you hot?

3. **Commands** — sentences which give orders or requests. (The subject of these sentences is usually understood and therefore not mentioned.)

    "(You) do not go out into the sun!"

4. **Exclamations** — sentences which express a strong feeling of emotion.

    My goodness, it's hot!

5. Greetings and sentences which don't have any definite form.

    **Good morning.
    Many happy returns.**

Simple sentences

A simple sentence has only *one* subject and *one* predicate.

> **The chef (subject) made a cake (predicate).**

It could take the form of a question:

> **Did the chef make a cake?**

or a command:

> **Make a cake!**

You can add any amount of adjectives[1] to the nouns:

> **The *jolly, fat* chef made an *enormous chocolate* cake.**

or any amount of adverbs[2] or adverbial phrases:[3]

> **The chef *happily* made a cake *in the kitchen after midnight.*
> (N.B. How? Where? When?)**

or both:

> **The jolly, fat chef happily made an enormous chocolate cake in the kitchen after midnight.**

Despite all the added description the sentence still has only *one subject* and *one verb*. It is still a simple sentence.

Compound sentences

If you used *simple* sentences all the time your writing and speech would sound very jerky. It is important to join sentences together to add variety to your language and make it flow.
    A *compound* sentence is made up of two or more simple sentences joined by a conjunction[4] or separated by a comma, semi-colon or colon.

Here are two simple sentences.

> **The ship hit the rocks.**

> **It sank to the bottom of the sea.**

If you join them together with the conjunction "and" you can make a compound sentence.

> **The ship hit the rocks and it sank to the bottom of the sea.**

or,

> **Jane likes swimming.**

> **Fred likes to play tennis.**

> **Tom does not like to do anything at all.**

Join them with commas and a conjunction:

> **Jane likes swimming, Fred likes to play tennis, but Tom does not like to do anything at all.**

Note that the separate parts of the compound sentence still make complete sense if you take away the conjunction or punctuation.

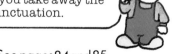

87

---

[1] See pages 72 and 73   [2] See page 80   [3] See page 88   [4] See pages 84 and 85

Phrases

A phrase is a group of words which does not make complete sense on its own and *does not* contain a verb. It is not a complete sentence.

up the mountain

This does not make complete sense.

If you add a subject and a verb to this phrase you can make a complete sentence.

The climber (subject)   **struggled (verb)**

The climber struggled up the mountain.

If you want to write longer and more interesting sentences you can use phrases instead of adjectives, nouns and adverbs.

Adjectival phrases

In these sentences the phrases are used instead of adjectives.

> **The man *with the bow-tie* danced with the lady *in the red dress*.**

> **Matilda, *refreshed by a long holiday in Greece*, felt she could dance all night.**

Can you see which nouns they are describing?

Adverbial phrases

In the sentences below the phrases act as adverbs answering the question *How? When?* and *Where?* about the verb.

The bull charged angrily *across the field*.

Can you see which phrases answer the question how?

They climbed over a gate *as soon as possible* and ran *like the wind*.

Noun phrases

These phrases are acting as nouns in the sentences. They can do *all* the things that nouns can do.

Here they are the subject of the sentences.

All the people in the audience began to clap at the brilliant speech.

The terrier with short ears was well-trained by his master.

Clauses

A clause is a group of words which *does* contain a verb. It is part of a sentence.

MAIN   **SUBORDINATE**

when she went shopping

This does not make sense.

If, however, you add another clause to the one above, it does make sense in the sentence.

This is another clause.

Sue bought a new dress when she went shopping.

Above there are two kinds of clauses: 1. *Main clause.* 2. *Subordinate clause.*

They are divided into two kinds according to the job they do in a sentence.

The most important clause is the *main clause.* This can stand by itself and make complete sense. It could be a sentence.

Richard ate five cream cakes

A *subordinate* clause is dependent on the main clause for its meaning.

because he was hungry

Clauses, like phrases, can do the work of adjectives, nouns and adverbs in a sentence. They make what you write more detailed and interesting.

Adjectival clause

These often begin with *who, which, that* or *whom.*

These are the nouns the clauses are describing.

The boy *who had the longest legs* won the race.

David was a person *whom everyone respected.*

Adverbial clause

An adverbial clause does the work of an adverb (i.e. it answers the questions How? When? Where? or Why?).

How?

He ran *as fast as he could.*

When?

They sang *as they walked along.*

Where?

Robbers break in *where they see valuables kept.*

Can you see which verbs the clauses are describing?

Why?

I missed the train *because I was late.*

Noun clause

A noun clause can take the place of a noun. It can be the *subject* or *object* of the verb.

Here it is the subject.

That there is life after death is impossible to prove.

I want to know *what you have been doing* all day.

Here it is the object.

89

Complex sentences

| SUBORDINATE | MAIN | SUBORDINATE |

A complex sentence is made up of a main clause[1] with one or more subordinate clauses.[2] Each clause always contains a verb.

The subordinate clauses can be noun, adjectival or adverbial clauses, and each one follows a preposition[3] or a conjunction.[4]

Look at the sentence below. The words in italics are verbs.

The man *limped* because his leg *hurt*.

The man *limped* (main clause)

> This makes sense on its own.

because his leg *hurt* (subordinate clause)

> This is an adverbial clause saying why he limped.

Now look at the next sentence. It has *two* subordinate clauses. Again, the verbs are in italics.

Rose, who *was* a greedy girl, *ate* five cakes when she *came* home from school.

Rose *ate* five cakes (main clause)

who *was* a greedy girl (subordinate clause)

> This is an adjectival clause describing Rose.

when she *came* home from school (subordinate clause)

Notice that each clause contains a verb.

> This is an adverbial clause modifying *ate*.

Subordinate clauses can come at the *beginning* or *end* of a sentence. The subordinate clauses below are in italics.

She took her dog with her *wherever she went*.

*Wherever she went* she took her dog with her.

You can have a subordinate clause at the beginning, the main clause in the middle and the other subordinate clause at the end.

When Tom got up he put on his brown suit, which was very smart.

> This is the main clause.

90

[1] See page 89. [2] See page 89. [3] See page 82. [4] See page 84.

Direct and reported speech

When you are writing sentences that contain somebody's speech you have to think carefully whether it is *direct* or *reported (indirect)* speech.

Direct speech

If you are writing down the exact words that someone is saying, or has said, it is called *direct* speech. The words actually spoken are put inside inverted commas (sometimes called quotation marks).

> **"I *am feeling* ill, Mum," said Fred.**

I am feeling ill.

> **"What *have* you *been eating*?" she asked.**

Reported (indirect) speech

You can, however, report what someone said in your own words. This is called *reported* or *indirect* speech. In this case you do not need inverted commas.

> **Fred told his Mum *he was feeling* ill.**

> **She asked him what *he had been eating*.**

Some of the verbs in the above sentences are in italics. These are the verbs included in the speech. If you look at the verbs in the *reported* speech you will notice that they are in the past tense. This is because you are writing down what happened in the past. The action is now over.

Direct speech — Remember the *tense* of each verb in reported speech goes back *one stage in time*.

Reported speech

> **"I *am* happy."** — (He said) he *was* happy.
> **"I *saw* it."** — (He said) he *had seen* it.

The future changes like this:

> **"I *shall* do it."** — (He said) he *would* do it.

Could you be a reporter?

Can you re-write Lady Bloggs' speech in your own words?

"Welcome everyone! It is wonderful to see so many of you here today supporting our Charity Bazaar. I do hope you will all give generously to this worthy cause. Last year we made two thousand pounds at the same event and I hope we may make *even* more this year. There are many stalls and attractions which I am sure you will find entertaining . . ."

91

Word order in sentences

The meaning of a sentence depends not only on the words you use but also the order in which they appear. Most of the time you put words in the right order without even having to think about it, but there are one or two tricky instances when it is easy to make mistakes.

Misplaced words

When you use common adverbs* you need to think quite carefully about where you place them. They should be immediately before the words they modify. The word *just* is a good example of one of these adverbs. Notice the difference in meaning between the sentences below.

I *just* told my mother what I had seen.	(I recently told my mother.)
I told *just* my mother what I had seen.	(I told only my mother.)
I told my mother *just* what I had seen.	(I told my mother exactly what I had seen.)
I told my mother what I had *just* seen.	(I told my mother what I had recently seen.)

Misplaced phrases

Sometimes whole phrases can get into the wrong position in a sentence. This can make the meaning unclear or ridiculous.

The teacher kept the child who misbehaved *in the corner.*

Did the child misbehave in the corner?

Or was the child kept in the corner because he misbehaved?

Try to put phrases as close as possible to the word or words they relate to most closely. This is particularly important when you are dealing with phrases that have verbs ending in "-ing" or "-ed".

We saw some poppies walking *round the field.*

Put this phrase at the beginning of the sentence. It describes "we", not the "poppies".

*See pages 80-81.

Misplaced clauses

Clauses which describe someone or something should be placed as near as possible to the person or thing they describe.

This word order makes it sound as though the cliffs were screeching.

I heard the seagulls near the cliffs *that were screeching.*

This clause needs to go nearer to the seagulls.

Split infinitives

An infinitive is the part of the verb that has "to" in front of it.

**to hop
to skip
to jump**

These are all infinitives.

It is nearly always a mistake to split "to" from the verb if you are using an infinitive.

The detective decided *to* slowly and carefully *study* the clues. X

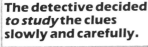

"To" and "study" should be next to each other.

The detective decided *to study* the clues slowly and carefully. ✓

Split verb and subject

The subject of a sentence should not be too far away from the verb because the meaning of the sentence can then become hard to follow.

***Albert,* after upsetting the basket and cracking all the eggs, *hid* in the cupboard.** X

"Albert" needs to be nearer "hid".

After upsetting the basket and cracking all the eggs, *Albert* hid in the cupboard. ✓

Wrong order

Can you spot the mistakes in the sentences below?:

1. I saw a frog fishing by the river.
2. The policeman arrested the man who was drunk quickly.
3. I saw the dog with its owner which was barking.
4. Ben, after eating ten chocolate bars, was sick.
5. She decided to gradually acquire a suntan.

Making the subject and verb agree

The subject of a sentence is who or what the sentence is about. It is in charge of or "governs" the verb. A singular subject means that the verb must be singular; a plural subject means that the verb must be plural.

(Singular subject)

This *cake is* stale.

(Singular verb)

These *cakes are* stale.

(Plural subject)

(Plural verb)

This is called making the subject and verb agree.

A group of words as a subject

If the subject is a group of words, rather than just one word, it is easy to make a mistake. Here the phrase "of potatoes" describing the subject can be mistaken for the subject itself.

A sack of potatoes *were* lying in the shed. X

(Subject phrase)

Decide which word is the subject by asking yourself *who* or *what* performed the action. Then think whether it is singular or plural and make the verb agree with it.

(Singular subject)

A *sack* of potatoes *was* lying in the shed. ✓

(Singular verb)

More than one verb

Sometimes one subject governs more than one verb. Make sure that all the verbs governed by a subject agree with it.

This *kind* of motorbike *looks* impressive but actually *do* not go very fast. X

(This should be *does* because the subject is "kind".)

(Don't make mistakes like this.)

Whenever you have difficulty deciding whether a verb should be singular or plural, find the subject and ask yourself whether it is singular or plural.

More common mistakes

1. Words like anyone, everyone, someone, no one, each (indefinite pronouns), are singular and should take a *singular* verb.

Everyone is going on a picnic today.

Singular verb

The words many, both, few and several always take a *plural* verb.

Several of us are going swimming.

Plural verb

2. When you use "neither ...nor" in a sentence it can be difficult to decide what to do with the verbs.

If both the subjects are singular use a singular verb.

Neither the dog nor the cat *likes* the way Tom plays his violin.

If one or both subjects are plural, the verb is plural.

Neither Ben nor his brothers *like* having a bath.

3. Collective nouns (words which describe groups of persons or things) usually take a *singular* verb.

**Class 4B
Ted's family
This football team
Tony's gang**
} **is** brilliant.

4. When a sentence has more than one subject joined by "and" the verb should be *plural*.

Here *come* Annie and her sister. ✓

Here *comes* Annie and her sister. ✗

There are two subjects so the verb is plural.

Spot the mistakes

Can you spot the wrong agreement in these sentences?

1. This dog are vicious.
2. These tomatoes is ripe.
3. A box of chocolates are sitting on the table.
4. Rod's gang are very large.
5. James and Lucy is going away today.
6. Neither Sid nor his friends is coming to my party.
7. Here comes the bride and groom.
8. Class 2B are very noisy.
9. Here are two apples: both is ripe.
10. A few of us *is* here.

Words easily confused

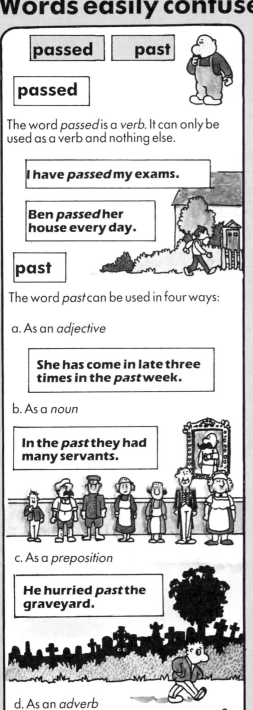

passed | past

passed

The word *passed* is a *verb*. It can only be used as a verb and nothing else.

> I have *passed* my exams.

> Ben *passed* her house every day.

past

The word *past* can be used in four ways:

a. As an *adjective*

> She has come in late three times in the *past* week.

b. As a *noun*

> In the *past* they had many servants.

c. As a *preposition*

> He hurried *past* the graveyard.

d. As an *adverb*

> The crowds cheered as the Queen went *past*.

off | of

These two words mean totally different things.

off

> "Get *off* my land!" shouted the farmer.

> She rubbed the dust *off* her shoes.

of

This sounds like *ov* when you say it because of the one "f".

> She climbed out *of* bed sleepily.

> Three *of* them wore hats.

Try not to confuse *of* with the word *have*.

Look at the sentence below:

> I *should have* gone with them.

Sometimes the words in italics are shortened to *should've*. This often sounds like *should of*.

Watch out for the words below:

could've (could have)
would've (would have)
might've (might have)
must've (must have)
may've (may have)

Never say or write *could of*, etc.

we're　were

we're

We're is a shortened form (contraction) of the pronoun *we* and the verb *are*.

> **We're going away tomorrow.**
> **We are going away tomorrow.**

were

This is part of the verb "to be". It is part of the past tense of the verb.

> **They *were* very happy to be going away.**

Helpful hint: If you cannot remember which of these words to use, think: "Can I replace it with two words?" If you *can*, you use the shortened form "we're". It's the same with "who's".

who's　whose

who's

This is the shortened form (contraction) of the pronoun *who*[1] and either the verb *is* or the verb *has*.

> **Who's (who is) coming to the party?**
> **Who's (who has) been drinking my wine?**

whose

This word can be two parts of speech:

a. A *relative pronoun*[2] which shows ownership on behalf of the noun it relates to.

> **This is the man *whose* dog bit me.**

"Whose" refers back to the noun "man".

b. A *possessive adjective*[3] which refers to the noun it is next to.

> **Whose dog is this?**

affect　effect

affect

The word *affect* is a verb which means "to cause a change in something".

> **Sue changed her job because it *affected* her health.**

effect

This is a noun which means "result" or "consequence".

> **The change in job had a good *effect* and she was no longer ill.**

but

The word *effect* is sometimes used as a verb which means "to bring something into being".

> **The doctor hoped he could *effect* a cure for the disease.**

97

[1]See pages 70-71　　[2]See page 71　　[3]See pages 72-73

Words often misused

teach | learn

teach

A teacher "teaches" someone how to do something. He gives out knowledge.

> **Jim is *teaching* me how to play the guitar.**

learn

This word means "to take in" knowledge.

> **I *learned* to play the guitar very quickly with Jim as a teacher.**

> You *cannot* "learn" someone how to do something.

lend | borrow

lend

This word means "to hand out" for a certain period of time.

> **"I will *lend* you a ruler," said Ben.**

borrow

This word means "to take from" for a certain period of time.

> **She *borrowed* Ben's ruler for a few minutes.**

> You lend *to* someone and borrow *from* someone.

saw | seen

saw

This word is a verb. It makes sense on its own.

> **I *saw* a film last night.**

seen

This word is only *part* of a verb. It needs an auxiliary verb* with it to help to make sense.

> **I *have seen* three films this week.**

You cannot write:

> **I *seen* three films this week.** ✗

did | done

did

The word *did* is a complete verb which makes sense on its own.

> **Dad *did* the washing.**

done

The word *done* is only part of a verb. It needs an auxiliary verb* to make sense.

> **Dad *has done* the washing.**

not

> **Dad *done* the washing.**

> "done" needs a *helping* verb with it.

✗

*See page 76

as | like

as

This word always needs a verb to follow it.

> **She did it *as* I *told* her to.**

like

This word is followed by a noun or pronoun only.

> **She looks *like* him.**

> **That man is driving *like* a madman.**

Do not write:

> **She did it *like* I told her to.** ✗

---

who | which

These words are relative pronouns.*
This means they take the place of a noun and join two phrases or clauses.
Who is always used to refer to people.
Which is always used to refer to animals or things.

who

Look at these two sentences:

> **I have two brothers.
> My brothers are fat.**

You can join these sentences together with a relative pronoun.

> **I have two brothers *who* are fat.**

"Who" takes the place of the noun "brothers".

which

The same applies to the word *which*.

> **She has three cats.
> The cats are Siamese.**

"Which" takes the place of the noun "cats".

> **She has three cats *which* are Siamese.**

---

can | may | might

can

This word means "capable of doing".

> **I *can* go out now.**

> **I *can* speak French well.**

may

This word is used in two ways:

1. To ask permission to do something.

> **May I go out now?**

Although nowadays people often say or write:

> **"*Can* we have lunch now?"** ✗

You *should* say:

> **"*May* we have lunch now?"**

2. You also use the word *may* when there is a fair possibility that something will happen.

> **The princess *may* visit this town tomorrow.**

This means it is quite possible.

might

This is used when there is less possibility of something happening.

> **The princess *might* visit this town tomorrow.**

This means there is a possibility but that it is not very likely.

*See page 71

Other problems

Here are some common mistakes which seem to crop up frequently in written and spoken English.

Slang

Everyone talks in "slang" sometimes. There are many words and phrases used in everyday speech and writing which are called slang. They are often funny expressions but should not be used in formal speech or writing.

Spot the slang

The sentences below are written in slang. Can you re-write them in formal English?

1. I'm fed up with this job, I'm going to pack it in.
2. John is keen on a bird up the road.
3. We thought Jane was stuck up but she was just feeling out of sorts.
4. Tim's father is in the nick because someone grassed on him.
5. Mum has flipped her lid because Bill has pushed off without telling her.
6. I'm so hard up I can't get to the movies.
7. Dad went round the bend when I told him to get lost.
8. She slogs her guts out working for a boss who's a pain in the neck.

Double negatives

A *negative* is a word which gives the meaning of "no" or "not". If you put *two* negatives in one sentence they will cancel each other out and you will lose the negative meaning altogether.

Look at this sentence:

X **I *don't* want *nothing*.**

There are *two* negatives here.

You should write:

I *don't* want anything. ✓

or

I want *nothing*. ✓

He's *not* seen *neither* of them. X

He's *not* seen either of them. ✓

or

He's seen *neither* of them. ✓

Jumping tenses

When you write a sentence or a passage you should always be consistent about the tense of the verb. If you start to write about something in the past, you must keep to the past all the way through. If you start to write in the present then you must continue in the present.

Look at the sentences below:

They walked through the forest and breathed in the scent of pine. It *is* cool and fresh and they *feel* as if they could stay forever.

What should the words in italics really be?

All the verbs are in the past tense except for *is* and *feel*. The tenses of these verbs have jumped to the present. This makes the passage rather confusing to the reader.

Odds and ends

hardly **scarcely**

When these words mean "no sooner than" they are always followed closely by *when* or *before*, not the word *than*.

He had scarcely left the house *when* the telephone rang.

No "than" here.

She had hardly eaten a mouthful *before* she felt sick.

them **those** Sometimes people use the word *them* as an adjective instead of *those*.

Them is the object form of the pronoun *they*. It can *never* be used as an adjective.

Give it to *them*.

Those can be used as a demonstrative adjective★ or as a pronoun. Here it is an adjective.

***Those* flowers are pretty.**

Do *not* write or say:

Pass me *them* books. X

It should be:

Pass me *those* books. √

between The word *between* is always followed by *and* not *or*.

She had a choice between a white dress *and* a black one. √

not

She had a choice between a white dress *or* a black one. X

to try *to* **to try *and*** You normally use the word *to* after the verb to try. It is a common mistake to put the word *and*.

√ **I am going to try *to* save money this year.**

X **I am going to try *and* save money this year.**

literally This word means "exactly to the letter" or "in actual fact". You *cannot* write:

Celia was *literally* rooted to the spot. X

This is possible.

You can write: √ **Celia literally fainted with shock.**

unique This word means the only one of its kind. You cannot say something is *quite* unique or *very* unique, it is either unique or not unique.

√ **This precious vase is *unique*.**

This precious vase is *quite* unique. X

★See pages 72-73

Tips on writing good English

Good writing should be clear, simple and concise. This does not mean that the sentences you write should be abrupt and full of short, uncomplicated words. It is important to use a variety of words and ways of expressing things. But it is also important to make sure that each word you use contributes something to the meaning of the sentence.

Planning

First of all it will help if you spend some time planning what you are going to write before you start writing. List all the points or ideas that you want to include and think carefully about how you are going to link or contrast them. Read through what you have planned, to see if you have forgotten anything.

Paragraphs

The way you arrange words on a page and the amount of space you leave around them also helps your reader to understand the exact meaning of your words.

Divide your writing into paragraphs to help your reader. A paragraph is a set of sentences. There is no rule about how many sentences there should be in a paragraph; just use as many as makes a digestible piece of reading. But do try to end one paragraph and begin another at a point where it is logical to have a slight break.

> The first line of a paragraph is set inwards from the margin (indented) to make it easier to see where each paragraph begins.

You usually start a new paragraph when introducing into the story:

1. A person

2. A new place.

3. A change of time.

4. A change of idea.

If you are writing down a conversation you always start a new paragraph every time one person stops speaking and another person starts. This makes it easier for the reader to tell who is speaking which words.

Take special care with the opening and closing paragraphs of what you write. The opening paragraph will decide whether you capture your reader's interest; the closing paragraph will determine the impression he is left with.

Reading through

> As you read through, you may also spot some spelling mistakes or missing punctuation.

When you have finished writing, read through what you have written. Think about your reader or readers. Try to put yourself in their position and see whether you can understand what you have written. Ask yourself whether it will hold their interest and whether it states accurately what you want to tell them.

Things to avoid

1. *Repetition.*

Your writing can become very boring for your reader if you keep repeating the same words or phrases unnecessarily.

> The same word is used too many times.

> **We visited a most *mysterious* house. There was a *mysterious* secret passage which led out to a walled garden. All the plants in the garden were white or grey which gave the place a very *mysterious* atmosphere.**

2. *Overworked words.*

Certain words tend to be used too much, so that their meaning becomes vague and woolly. They can be acceptable when used in just the right place, but it is better to think of a more precise alternative to replace them.

> nice lovely fantastic terrific great incredible horrible funny dreadful fine good get

> There are lots of other overworked words.

3. *Clichés.*

These are phrases that have been used over and over again until all their freshness and originality has disappeared. Try to think of your own way of expressing something instead of resorting to stock phrases.

> **In this day and age I think it is important for *each and every one of us, right across the board,* to *stand up and be counted.***

4. *Ambiguity.*

This is when there is more than one meaning to a sentence and there is no way of telling which one the writer intended. This often happens when a word or phrase is put in the wrong position.

> **The fire was put out before any damage could be done by the fire brigade.**

It can also happen when you use pronouns without making it quite clear to whom they refer.

> **If the baby does not eat its supper, throw it away.**

5. *Tautology.*

This is the use of an extra word or phrase which pointlessly repeats an idea in the sentence.

> **The annual party at Castle Crum is held every year.**

> "Annual" is the same as "every year".

You could say either:

> **There is an annual party at Castle Crum.**

or

> **The party at Castle Crum is held every year.**

6. *Verbosity.*

Using too many words where plain, straightforward language would be more effective, will make what you write sound pompous and unnatural. Try not to use long words where short ones are just as effective, or more words than are necessary to express your meaning.

> **At this moment in time I am of the opinion that it is of the utmost importance to labour diligently at whatsoever matter may fall to your lot.**

> **I now think that it is very important to work hard at whatever you do.**

Test yourself

How many pronouns?

Can you spot all the pronouns in these sentences?

Don't forget! There are different *kinds* of pronouns. See page 71.

1. I don't know which of them is going to help with this
2. She collected the parcel herself.
3. "To whom does that belong?" he asked angrily.
4. "These are ready, but those aren't," I said.
5. "Who do you think will be coming tonight?" she asked.
6. He has a car which he will lend us.

Which kind of noun?

In the eight sentences below there are 31 nouns. Can you find them all and decide which kind they are? (common, proper, collective or abstract?)

1. Everyone lived in fear of Charlie and his gang of thugs.
2. A flock of sheep ambled across the road, causing a huge traffic-jam.
3. Mary ran down the High Street to catch the bus, which was stopping outside the Odeon Cinema.
4. Claude was a Frenchman who came from Paris.
5. The jury took a long time to decide whether or not the prisoner had told the truth.
6. A fleet of ships sailed out of the harbour at great speed.
7. The farmer asked the vet to have a look at his herd of cows.
8. The crocodile gobbled up a shoal of fish.

See page 69 if you are stuck.

Comparing things

Can you fill in the missing words or letters below?

1. Jane is pretty but Sarah is even prett. . . .
2. Of the three boys, James is the fat. . . . .
3. My house is large, Tom's is larg . ., but Dan's house is the larg . . . .
4. John's behaviour is bad, but Tim's is . . . . .
5. The old lady had only a little money, her friend had even . . . . ., but the man round the corner had the . . . . . .

104

Phrase or clause?

In the sentences below, the words in italics form either a phrase or a clause. Can you sort out which is which?

Remember, a phrase does not have a verb in it.

1. The women *in the audience* began to faint.
2. They travelled wearily *across the desert*.
3. *When she was young* Doris was very attractive.
4. Tom ran *along the road, round the corner* and *into the house*.
5. James bought a new cassette *when he went shopping*.
6. The man *in the dark glasses* looked very mysterious.
7. Kim, *who is an eccentric person*, collects extremely unusual teapots.
8. Peter was a bully *whom everybody feared*.
9. Sue kept a goat *in her front garden*.

Spot the mistakes

There are 13 mistakes in the sentences below. Can you find them all?

1. "Who's book is this?" she asked.
2. "Whose coming to the party?" asked Sarah.
3. "I don't know whether these pills will have any affect," said the doctor.
4. She fell of her bicycle because off the hole in the road.
5. "You should of known better," said the teacher.
6. "Mum, will you learn me how to cook that dish?" she asked.
7. "Can I lend your car, Jim?" asked Jo.
8. "I seen four burglars come out of that house," she told the police.
9. Tom did the job like I told him to.
10. Jane done four hours' work last night.
11. She has four sisters which are all younger than her.
12. Henrietta has five white mice who are all female.

Participles quiz

Verb, adjective or noun? Can you work out how the participles have been used in the sentences below? (The participles are in italics.)

1. Alfie has *learnt* to walk already.
2. The acrobats performed an amazing *balancing* act.
3. The neighbours have *moved* out this week.
4. "That's seven years' bad luck," she said as she looked at the *broken* mirror.
5. *The fighting* in the playground worried the headmaster.
6. The *screaming* girls chased the filmstar down the road.
7. The baby next door is *teething*.
8. *The singing* in the chapel was a delight to her ears.

Missing prepositions

Can you think of suitable prepositions to fill the gaps below?

Charlie got . . . . early. He put . . . . his clothes and went . . . . the stairs . . . . the kitchen. He sat . . . . the table . . . . the window and looked . . . . the garden and saw his father sitting . . . . a tree. When he had finished eating he went . . . . the door, ... of the house and . . . . the garden to join his father. He sat . . . . him on the ground and looked seriously . . . . his eyes. "Can you lend me some money, Dad?" he asked.

What can you find?

There are 15 verbs, 27 adjectives and 10 adverbs in this story. Can you find them all?

In the middle of a dark, forbidding forest lived a strange, old man. His home was a rickety little shack which had two cracked windows and a creaking door.

The man lived quite alone except for the company of a thin, bedraggled cat, and a large, lazy dog.

Each day he wandered off among the tall pine-trees and whistled softly to himself. He only returned to his humble home late in the evening when the sun had gone down.

Then he would sit quietly by the flickering fire and warm his gnarled hands; or he would talk gently to the animals as he tossed them scraps of his meagre supper.

Despite his simple existence, the old man was content. He troubled no one, and no one troubled him.

Answers

Spot the noun (page 68)

Pick out the nouns

box
David
dog
cup
bottle

How many nouns?

18 nouns.

	Cynthia	rabbit	bicycle
	dress	budgerigar	man
Boris	Tom	Mary	bed
cat	dog	car	table
road	hamster	favour	chair

Find the pronouns (page 71)

1. She, them.
2. We, him, he.
3. I, this, yours, she.
4. You, her, she, us.
5. It, yours, it, mine.
6. They, me, them.

Spot the verb (page 76)

1. cleaned
2. is barking
3. has made
4. will be watching
5. has crashed
6. is tossing

Fill in the missing verb (page 76)

1. are
2. has
3. will
4. shall
5. will
6. is, *or* was
7. were, *or* are
   will be, have been.

Change around (page 77)

1. A huge, black spider *was eaten* by the cat.
2. The silver *is cleaned* by Doris every fortnight.
3. The lawn was *mowed* by Mum early this morning.
4. The money *was hidden* under the bed by the burglars.
5. The rubbish *was thrown* into the dustbin by Jo.
6. The horse *was brushed* by the groom.
7. The plants *are watered* by the gardener.
8. A taxi *was ordered* by him to take her home.

What is missing? (page 84)

1. because, as, since *or* while
2. but
3. whether, or
4. and, as well as.

Which pair? (page 84)

1. whether . . . or
2. not only . . . but also
3. either . . . or
4. neither . . . nor
5. both . . . and

Could you be a reporter? (page 91)

Possible answer: (Words in italics show change of tense.)

> Lady Bloggs *welcomed* everyone. She said that it *was* wonderful to see so many people there supporting their Charity Bazaar and *hoped* they *would* all give generously to the worthy cause. She went on to say that last year they *had made* two thousand pounds at the same event and *hoped* that they *might* make even more this year. There *were* many stalls and attractions which she *was* sure they *would* find entertaining.

Wrong order (page 93)

1. Fishing by the river, I saw a frog.
2. The policeman quickly arrested the man who was drunk.
3. I saw the dog which was barking, with its owner.
4. Ben was sick after eating ten chocolate bars.
5. She decided to acquire a suntan gradually.

Spot the mistakes (page 95)

1. This dog *is* vicious.
2. These tomatoes *are* ripe.
3. A box of chocolates *is* sitting on the table.
4. Rod's gang *is* very large.
5. James and Lucy *are* going away tomorrow.
6. Neither Sid nor his friends *are* coming to my party.
7. Here *come* the bride and groom.
8. Class 2B *is* very noisy.
9. Here are two apples: both *are* ripe.
10. A few of us *are* here.

How many pronouns? (page 104)

19 pronouns.
1. I, which, them, this.
2. She, herself.
3. Whom, that, he
4. These, those, I.
5. Who, you, she.
6. He, which, he, us.

Which kind of noun? (page 104)

1. *Common:* thugs, sheep, road, traffic-jam, bus, prisoner ships, harbour, farmer, vet, look, cows, crocodile, fish.
2. *Proper:* Charlie, Mary, High Street, Odeon Cinema, Claude, Frenchman, Paris.
3. *Collective:* gang, flock, jury, fleet, herd, shoal.
4. *Abstract:* fear, truth, speed, time.

Comparing things (page 104)

1. Jane is pretty but Sarah is even prett*ier*.
2. Of the three boys, James is the fatt*est*.
3. My house is large, Tom's is larg*er*, but Dan's house is the larg*est*.
4. John's behaviour is bad, but Tim's is *worse*.
5. The old lady had only a little money, her friend had even *less*, but the man round the corner had the *least*.

Phrase or clause (page 105)

1. phrase
2. phrase
3. clause
4. 3 phrases
5. clause
6. phrase
7. clause
8. clause
9. phrase

Spot the mistakes (page 105)

1. *Whose* book is this? she asked.
2. "*Who's* coming to the party?" asked Sarah.
3. "I don't know whether these pills will have any *effect*," said the doctor.
4. She fell *off* her bicycle because *of* the hole in the road.
5. "You should'*ve* (have) known better," said the teacher.
6. "Mum, will you *teach* me how to cook that dish?" she asked.
7. "Can I *borrow* your car, Jim?" asked Jo.
8. "I *saw* four burglars come out of that house," she told the police.
9. Tom did the job *as* I told him to.
10. Jane *did* four hours' work last night.
11. She has four sisters *who* are all younger than her.
12. Henrietta has five white mice *which* are all female.

Participles quiz (page 106)

1. verb
2. adjective
3. verb
4. adjective
5. noun (gerund)
6. adjective
7. verb
8. noun (gerund)

Missing prepositions (page 106)

up, on, down, into (to), at, by (near or beside), across (into), under, through, out, into, beside (near), into

What can you find (page 106)

Verbs – 14, lived (× 2), was, had, wandered, whistled, returned, had gone, would sit, warm, would talk, tossed, was, troubled (×2).

Adjectives – 27, dark, forbidding, strange, old (× 2), rickety, little, two, cracked, creaking, thin, bedraggled, large, lazy, each, tall, humble, flickering, gnarled, meagre, simple, content, his (× 5).

Adverbs – 10, quite, alone, off, softly, only, late, down, then, quietly, gently.

Literary terms – More tips on writing English

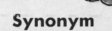

If you want to write in an interesting and lively way you may want to include some of the following:-

Similes

A simile compares two things, bringing out a point of "likeness" between the two things.

> **She was shaking like a leaf.**

The most common words which introduce a simile are:

> as, like, as if, as though, as . . . as.

Metaphors

A metaphor is like a simile except that it compares two things by saying that one thing *is* something else. It does not use the word "like" or "as".

> **That man is an ass.**

Alliteration

This is the repeating of a particular letter or sound (usually consonants at the beginning of words) to produce an interesting effect.

> **She sat sipping soda in the sizzling sun.**

Onomatopoeia

This is the use of words which imitate or suggest the sound of what they describe.

> **The ducks *quacked* and *splashed* in the water.**

> If you say these words aloud you can *hear* how similar they are to the noise they describe.

This use of words can intensify the meaning of what you write. It is often used in poetry.

Synonym

This is a word that has almost the same meaning as another word. Here are some

> small – tiny, little, minute

If you need to describe the same thing twice but want to avoid repetition you should use a synonym. It is a "stand-in" for the word it replaces.

> **Cynthia had *large* feet. In fact her feet were so *immense* she had to have *huge* shoes especially made for her.**

> If you use a synonym or an antonym it must be the same part of speech as the word it replaces.

Antonym

This is a word which has a meaning opposite to another word.

> slow – fast   work – relax

You may want to use an antonym to add a contrast in feeling or description.

> **All day Jane behaved like an *angel*, but her brother Sam was more like a *devil*.**

Index/glossary

Perennial Companio

PERENNIAL COMPANIONS

100 *Dazzling Plant Combinations for Every Season*

TOM FISCHER

Photographs by

RICHARD BLOOM & ADRIAN BLOOM

TIMBER PRESS
Portland • London

Published in 2009 by Timber Press, Inc.

The Haseltine Building
133 S.W. Second Avenue, Suite 450
Portland, Oregon 97204-3527
www.timberpress.com

2 The Quadrant
135 Salusbury Road
London NW6 6RJ
www.timberpress.co.uk

Printed in China

Library of Congress Cataloging-in-Publication Data

Fischer, Thomas, 1955–
  Perennnial Companions : 100 dazzling plant combina-
tions for every season / Tom Fischer ; photographs by
Richard Bloom and Adrian Bloom. — 1st ed.
    p. cm.
  Includes bibliographical references and index.
  ISBN 978-0-88192-939-3 (alk. paper)
1. Perennials. I. Bloom, Richard. II. Title.
  SB434.F57 2009
  635.9'32—dc22

                                    2008033296

A catalog record for this book is also available from the
British Library.

PHOTOGRAPHY, GARDEN, AND DESIGNER CREDITS

Photographs by Richard Bloom and Adrian Bloom.

Adrian's Wood, Bressingham Gardens, Norfolk, UK,
   Designed by Adrian Bloom, 128–29
The Bressingham Gardens, Norfolk, UK, 60–61
Chanticleer Garden, Wayne, PA, 78–79
The Dell Garden, Bressingham Gardens, Norfolk, UK,
   96–97, 108–9, 110–11, 154–55, 162–63, 166–67, 180–81,
   194–95
Eastgrove Cottage Garden Nursery, Worcestershire, UK,
   32–33
Foggy Bottom, Bressingham Gardens, Norfolk, UK,
   Designed by Adrian Bloom, 38–39, 54–55, 90–91,
   106–07, 136–37, 176–77, 196–97
Glen Chantry, Essex, UK, 36–37
Hullwood Barn, Suffolk, UK, 44–45
Lady Farm, Somerset, UK, designed by Judy Pearce,
   174–175
Merriments Garden, East Sussex, UK, 52–53
New York Botanical Garden, Bronx, NY, 144–45
The Picton Garden, Old Court Nurseries, Worcestershire,
   UK, 146–47, 160–61
RHS Wisley, Surrey, UK, Designed by Tom Stuart-Smith,
   170–71
Scampston Hall Garden, North Yorkshire, UK, Designed
   by Piet Oudolf, 76–77, 84–85, 98–99, 102–3, 116–17
Dennis Schrader's and Bill Smith's Garden, Mattituck, NY,
   120–21, 178–79
Tom Stuart-Smith, designer, 82–83
The Summer Garden, Bressingham Gardens, Norfolk, UK,
   Designed by Adrian Bloom, 86–87, 150–51, 164–65,
   172–73, 188–89, 206–7
The Thumbit, Suffolk, UK Designed by Ann James, 114–15

KEY TO PLANT CARE SYMBOLS

LIGHT REQUIREMENTS

SUN
Plant receives six hours or more of direct sun every day.

PART SUN
Plant receives three to six hours of direct sun every day.

LIGHT SHADE
Plant receives less than three hours of direct sun and gets dappled sun at other times during the day.

SHADE
Plant receives little or no direct sun, only dappled sun.

MOISTURE REQUIREMENTS

HEAVY
Plant needs constantly moist soil. Watering may be necessary during dry spells.

MODERATE
Plant needs moderate moisture. Occasional watering may be necessary during dry spells

LIGHT
Plant tolerates some dryness. Watering necessary only during prolonged drought or heat waves.

CONTENTS

INTRODUCTION

One of the greatest pleasures—and challenges—of gardening is combining plants to form pleasing juxtapositions of color, form, and texture. This is where your creativity kicks in, where you can start to have fun after all those hours of weeding, watering, and soil preparation. And perennials are the ideal medium for this kind of experimentation, since they're easy to obtain (usually), small enough to move around the garden if necessary, and endlessly varied in their visual qualities. The choices are nearly infinite.

Which is precisely the problem. There are so many choices that it can be hard to decide where to begin. This book is intended to help you get going, to show you actual combinations you might want to try (or modify) in your own garden. It's primarily visual inspiration. Basic cultural information is included for each combination: light and water requirements, and the height, spread, and hardiness zones for every plant. But keep in mind that you can always find more detailed information (such as propagation methods) online. The Internet is also the place to find sources for a particular plant that strikes your fancy. Remember, even if you can't find a specific cultivar, you can almost always find another that's similar in color or habit.

The one hundred combinations in this book take you from spring through summer and autumn and into winter. This chronological arrangement is meant to show that a garden well stocked with perennials can look attractive at any time of year—you just need to make the right plant choices.

I hope that, in these pages, you'll find combinations that will stimulate your imagination and encourage you to try something new in your garden—to boldly go . . . well, you get the idea. Happy gardening.

1. Lenten rose (*Helleborus* ×*hybridus*)
Height/Spread: 12–18 in. × 12–30 in.
Hardy in zones 4–9

2. Golden wood rush (*Luzula sylvatica* 'Aurea')
Height/Spread: 24 in. × 18 in.
Hardy in zones 4–9

3. 'Frühlingshimmel' lungwort (*Pulmonaria saccharata* 'Frühlings-himmel')
Height/Spread: 8–10 in. × 18 in.
Hardy in zones 3–9

4. Five-leaved cuckoo flower (*Cardamine quinquefolia*)
Height/Spread: 9 in. × 6 in.
Hardy in zones 5–9

Delicate tints of cream, chartreuse, and lilac gently welcome the new gardening year. (Later, they might look somewhat insipid.) For summer color, you can interplant later-emerging perennials, like hardy geraniums, among the cuckoo flower. (Actually, it's more fun to use the botanical name for this plant—it sounds like a cussword: car-DAM-ih-nee.)

1. Lenten rose (*Helleborus* ×*hybridus*)
Height/Spread: 12–18 in. × 12–30 in.
Hardy in zones 4–9

2. 'Lewis Palmer' lungwort (*Pulmonaria* 'Lewis Palmer')
Height/Spread: 9–18 in. × 12–18 in.
Hardy in zones 4–8

Lenten roses come in a wide range of colors, and the deep, glowing pink of this one looks good enough to eat, but don't—all hellebores are highly poisonous. That doesn't mean you shouldn't plant them in the garden; just be careful, and surround them with plenty of nice pastels to bring out their deep color.

1. Primrose (*Primula vulgaris*)
Height/Spread: 5–9 in. × 9 in.
Hardy in zones 5–8

2. 'La Grave' periwinkle (*Vinca minor* 'La Grave')
Height/Spread: 6–10 in. × 18 in. (spreading)
Hardy in zones 4–9

Periwinkle is well known as an easy, vigorous (some might say *too* vigorous) groundcover. There's no denying, however, that the large, blue-lavender flowers of the selection 'La Grave' are quite an eyeful; they find their perfect complement in the fragrant, pale-lemon blossoms of common primrose.

1. 'Santa Fe' peony (*Paeonia lactiflora* 'Santa Fe')
Height/Spread: 32 in. × 36 in.
Hardy in zones 3–8

2. Glory-of-the-snow (*Chionodoxa forbesii*)
Height/Spread: 5–10 in. × 4 in.
Hardy in zones 3–8

The emerging foliage of peonies can be as spectacular as the flowers and greatly extends the plant's season of interest. Planted among the vivid blue of the glory-of-the-snow, it practically glows. In late spring, 'Santa Fe' peony bears bright cerise flowers with a fluffy, creamy white center.

1. Toadshade (*Trillium sessile*)
Height/Spread: 4–10 in. × 12 in.
Hardy in zones 4–9

2. Starflower (*Ipheion uniflorum*)
Height/Spread: 3–5 in. × 2–3 in.
Hardy in zones 5–9

3. False oxlip (*Primula veris* × *Primula vulgaris*)
Height/Spread: 8–12 in. × 9 in.
Hardy in zones 3–8

The rich garnet red of toadshade (terrible name, wonderful plant; a trillium, in fact) finds a perfect foil in the pastels of the starflower and oxlip. These plants all thrive in the shade of deciduous trees, in soil with plenty of leaf mold or compost. Don't cut back the starflower foliage until it starts to turn yellow.

1. Golden-edged Dalmatian iris (*Iris pallida* 'Variegata')
Height/Spread: 24–30 in. × 12 in.
Hardy in zones 4–9

2. 'Jan Reus' tulip (*Tulipa* 'Jan Reus')
Height/Spread: 18 in. × 6–8 in.
Hardy in zones 3–8

3. Cushion spurge (*Euphorbia polychroma*)
Height/Spread: 12–18 in. × 18–36 in.
Hardy in zones 4–7

A study in effective contrasts: the linearity of the Dalmatian iris finds its perfect complement in the bright chartreuse mounds of the cushion spurge and the deep maroon chalices of the tulip. Although you could use a different tulip, it should be dark, to keep the composition crisp and emphatic.

1. Red-leaved barrenwort (*Epimedium ×rubrum*)

Height/Spread: 12 in. × 12–16 in.
Hardy in zones 4–9

2. 'Lewis Palmer' lungwort (*Pulmonaria* 'Lewis Palmer')

Height/Spread: 9–18 in. × 12–18 in.
Hardy in zones 4–8

Sometimes a gamble pays off: the pink and lavender flowers of the lungwort and the coppery red leaves of the barrenwort might not seem like an obvious pairing, but the results prove that it can be exciting to break the "color rules." It feels *great* to be a garden outlaw.

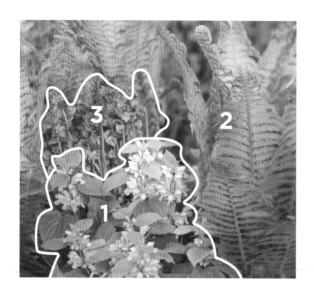

1. White-flowered deadnettle (*Lamium orvala* 'Album')
Height/Spread: 26 in. × 32 in.
Hardy in zones 4–9

2. Ostrich fern (*Matteuccia struthiopteris*)
Height/Spread: 36–72 in. × 60–96 in.
Hardy in zones 3–8

3. English bluebell (*Hyacinthoides non-scripta*)
Height/Spread: 8–12 in. × 4–6 in.
Hardy in zones 4–9

Blue, white, and chartreuse make a fail-safe combination, whether in sun or in shade. The fern and deadnettle are both vigorous plants; the expanding fern fronds can hide the bluebell's less-than-appealing foliage once it's done flowering. Gardens are like houses—they rarely stay neat for long.

**1. 'Frances Williams' hosta
(*Hosta* 'Frances Williams')**
Height/Spread: 22–24 in. × 48 in.
Hardy in zones 3–10

**2. Double white wood anemone
(*Anemone nemorosa* 'Alba Plena')**
Height/Spread: 6 in. × 8 in.
Hardy in zones 4–8

'Frances Williams' is one of the truly great classic hostas, with exceptional heat tolerance and boldly margined blue-green leaves. In spring, it can serve as a sculptural counterpoint to a carpet of charming wood anemones, which will disappear as the hosta's foliage expands.

1. Bicolor barrenwort (*Epimedium ×versicolor*)
Height/Spread: 6–15 in. × 9–18 in.
Hardy in zones 5–9

2. 'Heavenly Blue' lithodora (*Lithodora diffusa* 'Heavenly Blue')
Height/Spread: 6 in. × 12–20 in.
Hardy in zones 6–8

Juxtaposing mound-shaped plants with low ground-covers can be a highly effective design strategy. Here, this approach is even more successful thanks to the pleasing contrast between the blue lithodora flowers and the red-tinted barrenwort foliage.

1. Crested royal fern (*Osmunda regalis* 'Cristata')
Height/Spread: 48–60 in. × 36–48 in.
Hardy in zones 4–9

2. Wake robin (*Trillium erectum*)
Height/Spread: 8–18 in. × 9–12 in.
Hardy in zones 2–8

Seasoned gardeners know that perennials can be appealing at every stage of their yearly cycle: early growth, maturity, and decline. This combination exploits the strange yet intriguing appearance of unfurling crested royal fern fronds, before they have reached their majestic fullness. The demure wake robin underscores the linearity of the fern, which could have come from one of Dr. Seuss's books.

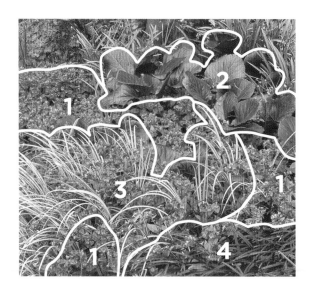

1. Blue lungwort (*Pulmonaria angustifolia* subsp. *azurea*)
Height/Spread: 10 in. × 16 in.
Hardy in zones 4–8

2. 'Bressingham Ruby' heartleaf bergenia (*Bergenia* 'Bressingham Ruby')
Height/Spread: 14 in. × 12 in.
Hardy in zones 3–10

3. Golden Japanese sweet flag (*Acorus gramineus* 'Ogon')
Height/Spread: 12 in. × 24 in.
Hardy in zones 7–10

4. Black mondo grass (*Ophiopogon planiscapus* 'Nigrescens')
Height/Spread: 9–12 in. × 9–12 in.
Hardy in zones 6–9

Foliage rules here, with the dazzling yellow of the Japanese sweet flag playing off the jet black of the mondo grass. The reddish bergenia leaves provide dramatic contrast, while the purple pulmonaria ties it all together, making for an intriguing blend of leaf and blossom.

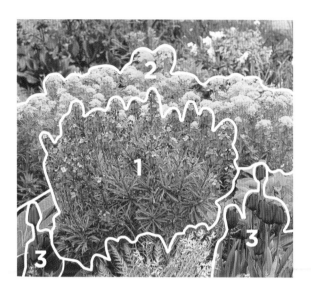

1. 'Bowles' Mauve' wallflower (*Erysimum* 'Bowles' Mauve')

Height/Spread: 24–32 in. × 18–24 in.
Hardy in zones 6–10

2. Marsh spurge (*Euphorbia palustris*)

Height/Spread: 24–36 in. × 36–48 in.
Hardy in zones 5–8

3. 'Jan Reus' tulip (*Tulipa* 'Jan Reus')

Height/Spread: 18 in. × 6–8 in.
Hardy in zones 3–8

The bright lavender wallflower here isn't exactly shy—nor is the spurge, with its startling chartreuse flower heads. The maroon 'Jan Reus' tulips keep the others from seeming garish. On the other hand, you could push things to the limit by planting a scarlet-flowered tulip. Now *that* would cause comment!

1. 'Bacchanal' western bleeding heart (*Dicentra* 'Bacchanal')
Height/Spread: 12–18 in. × 12–18 in.
Hardy in zones 3–9

2. 'Dahlem' soft shield fern (*Polystichum setiferum* 'Dahlem')
Height/Spread: 24–36 in. × 36 in.
Hardy in zones 5–8

3. Double bloodroot (*Sanguinaria canadensis* f. *multiplex*)
Height/Spread: 6–8 in. × 12 in.
Hardy in zones 3–9

The foliage of 'Bacchanal' bleeding heart could easily be mistaken for a fern; later in spring it will bear deep rose flowers. The furry crosiers of 'Dahlem' soft shield fern will later expand into majestic, arching fronds. Double bloodroot serves as a delicate counterpoint to the greenery.

1. 'West Point' tulip (*Tulipa* 'West Point')
Height/Spread: 20 in. × 8–10 in.
Hardy in zones 3–8

2. 'Spinners' hosta (*Hosta* 'Spinners')
Height/Spread: 24 in. × 32 in.
Hardy in zones 3–10

3. Caucasian peony (*Paeonia mlokosewitschii*)
Height/Spread: 24–36 in. × 24–36 in.
Hardy in zones 3–8

Yellow never fails to cheer, whether as the rich cream of Caucasian peony or the assertive lemon of 'West Point' tulips. Although the peony's flowers are short-lived, the plant also offers handsome foliage, as does the boldly margined hosta. Notice how the shape of the tulip's flowers mirrors the expanding hosta leaves. Neat, huh?

1. 'Purple Leaf' corydalis (*Corydalis flexuosa* 'Purple Leaf')
Height/Spread: 8–12 in. × 8 in.
Hardy in zones 5–8

2. Toadshade (*Trillium sessile*)
Height/Spread: 4–10 in. × 12 in.
Hardy in zones 4–9

3. Western white trillium (*Trillium ovatum*)
Height/Spread: 6–24 in. × 16–20 in.
Hardy in zones 5–9

4. 'Pearl Drops' western bleeding heart (*Dicentra* 'Pearl Drops')
Height/Spread: 12–16 in. × 16 in.
Hardy in zones 4–8

The small, bright, abundant flowers featured in this combination create an effect reminiscent of the charming millefleur (French for "thousand flowers") motifs in Renaissance tapestries. Of course, if you've never seen a millefleur tapestry, the point is lost. Trust me, they're nice.

1. 'Silver Swan' Mediterranean spurge (*Euphorbia characias* 'Silver Swan')
Height/Spread: 28 in. × 30 in.
Hardy in zones 7–10

2. Honesty (*Lunaria annua*)
Height/Spread: 20–36 in. × 12–24 in.
Hardy in zones 4–8

Variegated foliage—like that of 'Silver Swan' spurge—can be every bit as eye-catching as a showy floral display. That said, a little goes a long way. Here, it brings out the rich, rosy lavender of the honesty. Both plants will withstand dry soil in summer. Although honesty is a biennial, it usually seeds itself (sometimes excessively), so you'll rarely be without it.

1. 'Pearl Drops' western bleeding heart (*Dicentra* 'Pearl Drops')
Height/Spread: 12–16 in. × 16 in.
Hardy in zones 4–8

2. 'Cherry Ingram' Venus' navelwort (*Omphalodes cappadocica* 'Cherry Ingram')
Height/Spread: 10 in. × 15 in.
Hardy in zones 6–9

This pairing is a harmony made in horticultural heaven. The bright blue of the navelwort couldn't have a better partner than the blush-white flowers and ferny, blue-green foliage of the bleeding heart. Plant this duo in a shady spot and then spend the rest of the day feeling smug.

1. Siberian wallflower (*Erysimum ×marshallii*)

Height/Spread: 14–24 in. × 6–8 in.
Hardy in zones 5–9

2. 'Purple Sensation' ornamental onion (*Allium hollandicum* 'Purple Sensation')

Height/Spread: 20–30 in.; S; 12 in.
Hardy in zones 3–8

3. 'Blue Jacket' lupine (*Lupinus* 'Blue Jacket')

Height/Spread: 30–36 in. × 18 in.
Hardy in zones 4–8

Purple and orange? Sure—why not! Unless you take chances with color, you'll never experience the pleasure that a truly outrageous combination can give. The boldly contrasting shapes ensure that this particular grouping will be imprinted on your retina forever.

1. 'Forescate' chives (*Allium schoen-oprasum* 'Forescate')

Height/Spread: 12–15 in. × 15 in.
Hardy in zones 3–9

2. Gold-variegated Japanese forest grass (*Hakonechloa macra* 'Aureola')

Height/Spread: 14 in. × 18–24 in.
Hardy in zones 5–8

3. 'Porlock' thyme (*Thymus* 'Porlock')

Height/Spread: 10 in. × 10 in.
Hardy in zones 5–9

Many plants that we think of as culinary herbs are attractive enough to be used in the perennial garden. Here, 'Forescate' chives, a selection with particularly vivid flowers, makes a zingy companion for delicate 'Porlock' thyme and elegant Japanese forest grass.

1. Common columbine (*Aquilegia vulgaris*)
Height/Spread: 24 in. × 15 in.
Hardy in zones 4–9

2. Perfoliate alexanders (*Smyrnium perfoliatum*)
Height/Spread: 18–36 in. × 18 in.
Hardy in zones 5–8

Common columbine comes in a rainbow of colors, but when you've got a really good, deep purple strain, a chartreuse-flowered plant is just the thing to bring out the columbine's rich hue. Perfoliate alexanders is actually a biennial (or triennial) that takes two to three years to reach mature size and then dies after blooming. Let it seed around if you want it to be a permanent denizen of your garden (ditto with the columbine).

1. 'Quechee' tall bearded iris (*Iris* 'Quechee')
Height/Spread: 36 in. × 18 in.
Hardy in zones 3–10

2. 'Dropmore' catmint (*Nepeta* 'Dropmore')
Height/Spread: 18 in. × 12–18 in.
Hardy in zones 3–8

The color of 'Quechee' is remarkable among bearded iris—a sumptuous, deep orange-red. If you could find silk in that color, you'd want to wear something made out of it. The small violet-blue flowers of the catmint deftly underscore the smoldering iris. This pairing would be ideal for dry, sunny gardens.

1. 'Superba' bistort (*Persicaria bistorta* 'Superba')
Height/Spread: 24–30 in. × 24 in.
Hardy in zones 4–8

2. 'Tall Boy' cypress spurge (*Euphorbia cyparissias* 'Tall Boy')
Height/Spread: 9–12 in. × 12–18 in.
Hardy in zones 4–8

This pairing is undeniably handsome, and both plants stay in bloom for months, but don't attempt it unless you need to cover a lot of ground—both bistort and cypress spurge are vigorous spreaders—and can offer evenly moist soil. (Note: cypress spurge is considered invasive in most of the New England and Mid-Atlantic states and in Colorado.)

1. 'Halcyon' hosta (*Hosta* 'Halcyon')
Height/Spread: 20 in. × 24–30 in.
Hardy in zones 3–8

2. Bowles' golden sedge (*Carex elata* 'Aurea')
Height/Spread: 18–30 in. × 18–30 in.
Hardy in zones 5–9

3. Royal fern (*Osmunda regalis*)
Height/Spread: 48–60 in. × 36–48 in.
Hardy in zones 4–9

4. White-flowered bigroot cranesbill (*Geranium macrorrhizum* 'Album')
Height/Spread: 14 in. × 32 in.
Hardy in zones 3–8

Hostas are indispensable, reliable plants, but they need partners with contrasting shapes and textures; otherwise, they look boring and lumpy. The sedge, fern, and cranesbill do the trick here, with the sedge offering grassy foliage and the others providing airy, finely divided foliage. Plus the gold of the sedge looks great with the blue hosta leaves.

1. 'Majesté' lungwort (*Pulmonaria* 'Majesté')

Height/Spread: 8–12 in. × 12–18 in.
Hardy in zones 3–9

2. 'Leopard' lungwort (*Pulmonaria saccharata* 'Leopard')

Height/Spread: 12–18 in. × 18–24 in.
Hardy in zones 3–9

3. Bowles' golden sedge (*Carex elata* 'Aurea')

Height/Spread: 18–30 in. × 18–30 in.
Hardy in zones 5–9

Here is proof that foliage alone can create a satisfying garden scene. After the lungworts have finished flowering, their leaves remain attractive for the rest of the growing season. (Hint: if they look tattered or mildewed after flowering, cut them back to the ground for a flush of healthy new growth that will last for months.) The grasslike sedge adds a welcome bright note.

1. 'Canon Went' toadflax (*Linaria purpurea* 'Canon Went')
Height/Spread: 24–36 in. × 18–24 in.
Hardy in zones 5–8

2. White peach-leaved bellflower (*Campanula persicifolia* var. *alba*)
Height/Spread: 24–36 in. × 12–15 in.
Hardy in zones 3–8

3. 'Friedrich Hahn' beardtongue (*Penstemon* 'Andenken an Friedrich Hahn')
Height/Spread: 12–24 in. × 12–24 in.
Hardy in zones 7–9
(treat as annual in colder areas)

It's easy to create a harmonious color grouping if you combine white, a saturated hue (like red), and the tint that results when you mix white with the saturated hue (in this case, pink). These three plants all have slender, upright stems and so give an impression of grace and delicacy.

1. 'Prince' alumroot (*Heuchera* 'Prince')
Height/Spread: 16 in. × 15 in.
Hardy in zones 5–9

2. 'Silver Scrolls' alumroot (*Heuchera* 'Silver Scrolls')
Height/Spread: 12 in. × 12 in.
Hardy in zones 5–9

2. 'Hort's Variety' flower of Jove (*Lychnis flos-jovis* 'Hort's Variety')
Height/Spread: 12 in. × 16 in.
Hardy in zones 3–9

4. 'Blue Waterfall' Serbian bellflower (*Campanula poscharskyana* 'Blue Waterfall')
Height/Spread: 8–10 in. × 20–24 in.
Hardy in zones 4–8

In all honesty, this is probably as complicated a grouping as you should ever attempt. Even though there is a profusion of plant shapes and flower colors, the two alumroots manage to prevent things from degenerating into chaos. So remember: When in doubt, use multiples of the same plant.

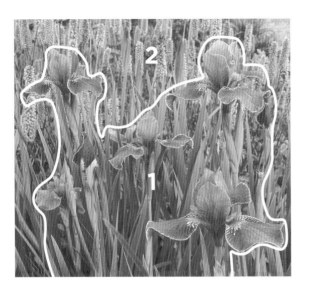

1. 'Silver Edge' Siberian iris (*Iris sibirica* 'Silver Edge')
Height/Spread: 30 in. × 30 in.
Hardy in zones 3–9

2. 'Hohe Tatra' bistort (*Persicaria bistorta* 'Hohe Tatra')
Height/Spread: 24–28 in. × 24–36 in.
Hardy in zones 4–8

Sometimes you just want pretty, soothing color, and that's what this combination delivers. 'Hohe Tatra' is a compact, vividly colored selection of bistort, and it provides just the right degree of warmth for the cool, violet-blue iris. Both plants will be happier in soil that never gets too dry.

**1. 'Peter Pan' Oriental poppy
(*Papaver orientale* 'Peter Pan')**
Height/Spread: 10–12 in. × 12–16 in.
Hardy in zones 3–8

**2. 'Lauren's Lilac' Oriental poppy
(*Papaver orientale* 'Lauren's Lilac')**
Height/Spread: 24–36 in. × 18–24 in.
Hardy in zones 3–8

**3. 'Shirley Pope' Siberian iris
(*Iris sibirica* 'Shirley Pope')**
Height/Spread: 36 in. × 24 in.
Hardy in zones 3–9

Oriental poppies come in a range of dazzling reds, pinks, and oranges, as well as pure white and lavender. Serendipitously, they bloom at the same time as Siberian iris, in one of the true climaxes of the gardening year. Keep in mind that Oriental poppies go dormant after they finish blooming, so it's wise to plant something nearby (like a perennial sunflower) that matures later in the summer.

1. 'Walther Funcke' yarrow (*Achillea* 'Walther Funcke')

Height/Spread: 14–24 in. × 14–18 in.
Hardy in zones 3–9

2. 'Blue Cloud' cranesbill (*Geranium* 'Blue Cloud')

Height/Spread: 9–12 in. × 12–24 in.
Hardy in zones 5–8

OK, maybe the name is a little hard to pronounce (say "VAL-tur FOONK-uh"), but few other perennials pack as much pure color punch as 'Walther Funcke' yarrow. In fact, you'll probably want to tone it down a little, which is why the pale blue-lilac cranesbill makes such a good partner. Or you could just reach for your sunglasses.

1. White wood cranesbill (*Geranium sylvaticum* 'Album')
Height/Spread: 24 in. × 12 in.
Hardy in zones 4–8

2. Himalayan cranesbill (*Geranium himalayense*)
Height/Spread: 12–16 in. × 18–24 in.
Hardy in zones 4–8

3. Crested golden-scaled male fern (*Dryopteris affinis* 'Cristata')
Height/Spread: 36–48 in. × 36 in.
Hardy in zones 5–9

Cranesbills are wonderfully collectable. Their flowers come in a range of pinks, purples, whites, and blues, and they have large, handsomely lobed leaves that make a visual contribution to the garden both before and after the plants have bloomed. Combine any two (or three or four or more) and you get instant harmony.

1. Masterwort (*Astrantia maxima*)
Height/Spread: 24 in. × 12 in.
Hardy in zones 4–8

2. 'Blue Cloud' cranesbill (*Geranium* 'Blue Cloud')
Height/Spread: 9–12 in. × 12–24 in.
Hardy in zones 5–8

Masterwort's appeal is twofold: the color is a clear mid-pink, leaning neither toward coral nor magenta, and the flower form is enchantingly intricate. Companions therefore need to be simple in outline and subdued in color, hence the 'Blue Cloud' cranesbill.

1. 'Chandelier' lupine (*Lupinus* 'Chandelier')
Height/Spread: 36 in. × 24 in.
Hardy in zones 4–8

2. White meadow cranesbill (*Geranium pratense* 'Album')
Height/Spread: 24 in. × 24 in.
Hardy in zones 3–8

If you want instant sparkle, trying pairing yellow and white. Here, this most cheerful of combinations gets an extra boost from the soaring, rocket-like spires of the lupine. If you're feeling adventurous, try partnering pink, white, or purple lupines with other cranesbills. It'll be hard to go wrong.

1. 'Helen Jane' cinquefoil (*Potentilla* 'Helen Jane')
Height/Spread: 18 in. × 18 in.
Hardy in zones 5–8

2. 'Silver Queen' white sage (*Artemisia ludoviciana* 'Silver Queen')
Height/Spread: 24 in. × 24 in. (spreading)
Hardy in zones 4–9

An excellent groundcover, 'Silver Queen' white sage will spread vigorously in some gardens, so be forewarned. Its icy gray-white foliage makes a perfect backdrop for the bright rosy pink cinquefoil, which is easily raised from seed. The herbaceous cinquefoils have an airy charm that many of their shrubby kin lack.

1. 'Hummelo' betony (*Stachys officinalis* 'Hummelo')

Height/Spread: 18–24 in. × 18–24 in.
Hardy in zones 4–8

2. Hardy Jerusalem sage (*Phlomis russeliana*)

Height/Spread: 36 in. × 20 in.
Hardy in zones 4–10

3. 'Rehbraun' panic grass (*Panicum virgatum* 'Rehbraun')

Height/Spread: 48 in. × 18 in.
Hardy in zones 4–8

4. 'Scorpion' beebalm (*Monarda* 'Scorpion')

Height/Spread: 36 in. × 24 in.
Hardy in zones 3–9

Magenta used to be banned from all gardens with pretensions to taste, but fortunately that bit of silliness has withered away. As is clear from this combination, magenta is a splendidly rich color, especially when used en masse. The lemon clusters of the hardy Jerusalem sage make a perfect accent/foil/second banana.

1. Century plant (*Agave americana*)
Height/Spread: 36–60 in. × 48–96 in.
Hardy in zones 7/8–10

2. Double soapwort (*Saponaria officinalis* 'Flore Pleno')
Height/Spread: 12–24 in. × 12–18 in.
Hardy in zones 3–8

3. Spiny bear's breeches (*Acanthus spinosus*)
Height/Spread: 36–48 in. × 36–48 in.
Hardy in zones 5–9

4. African honey bush (*Melianthus major*)
Height/Spread: 72 in. × 72 in.
Hardy in zones 8–10

Dramatic forms and foliage abound in this combination. In colder areas, the agave and honey bush will need to be grown in containers and overwintered indoors. (A quick Internet search will turn up other *Agave* species hardy to zone 6.) For all these plants, excellent drainage is a must.

1. 'Chocolate Ruffles' alumroot (*Heuchera* 'Chocolate Ruffles')
Height/Spread: 12–24 in. × 12–18 in.
Hardy in zones 4–9

2. Blonde sedge (*Carex albula*)
Height/Spread: 10–18 in. × 24 in.
Hardy in zones 7–10

This elegant, understated pairing could well be called "chocolate and vanilla," since the sedge's leaves become nearly white as they mature. If eye-popping color is what you're after, look elsewhere, but if long-lasting elegance appeals to you, then these plants fit the bill.

1. Persian onion (*Allium cristophii*)
Height/Spread: 24–36 in. × 12 in.
Hardy in zones 4–8

2. Armenian cranesbill (*Geranium psilostemon*)
Height/Spread: 30–48 in. × 36–48 in.
Hardy in zones 5–8

3. 'Husker Red' beardtongue (*Penstemon digitalis* 'Husker Red')
Height/Spread: 24–36 in. × 12–24 in.
Hardy in zones 3–8

Dusky purples—whether they occur in flowers or foliage—are among the best mixers in the garden, toning down harsh colors and making pastels seem brighter. This combination stays attractive for many weeks, with the onion forming intricate seed heads and the beardtongue producing delicate pinkish-white flowers.

1. 'Amethyst' meadow sage (*Salvia nemorosa* 'Amethyst')
Height/Spread: 24–30 in. × 28–36 in.
Hardy in zones 4–9

2. Autumn moor grass (*Sesleria autumnalis*)
Height/Spread: 12–36 in. × 12–36 in.
Hardy in zones 5–8

3. 'Bressingham's Delight' cranesbill (*Geranium* ×*oxonianum* 'Bressingham's Delight')
Height/Spread: 12–18 in. × 12–24 in.
Hardy in zones 5–9

4. Pale purple coneflower (*Echinacea pallida*)
Height/Spread: 24–36 in. × 12–18 in.
Hardy in zones 3–10

5. 'Scorpion' beebalm (*Monarda* 'Scorpion')
Height/Spread: 36 in. × 24 in.
Hardy in zones 3–9

Taking a single hue—in this case rosy purple—and seeing how far you can go with it can be both fun and challenging. The trick is to get lots of contrasting shapes—daisies, spikes, dense clusters, and so on—and then throw in a striking foliage plant that sets off the prevailing floral color.

1. 'Rozanne' cranesbill (*Geranium* 'Rozanne')
Height/Spread: 18–20 in. × 18–24 in.
Hardy in zones 5–8

2. 'Loraine Sunshine' ox-eye (*Heliopsis* 'Loraine Sunshine')
Height/Spread: 30 in. × 16 in.
Hardy in zones 4–9

'Rozanne' is one of the longest-blooming and most floriferous cranesbills ever bred, and so can be used in combinations that run from early to late summer. It's particularly effective used in large drifts to produce a river of purple-blue blossoms. Kind of makes you want to go for a swim, doesn't it?

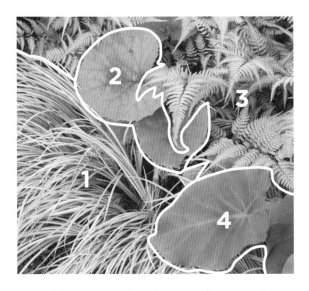

1. Golden Japanese sweet flag (*Acorus gramineus* 'Ogon')
Height/Spread: 12 in. × 24 in.
Hardy in zones 7–10

2. Butterbur (*Petasites hybridus*)
Height/Spread: 24–36 in. × 36–48 in.
Hardy in zones 4–9

3. Japanese painted fern (*Athyrium niponicum* 'Pictum')
Height/Spread: 12–18 in. × 18–24 in.
Hardy in zones 3–8

4. Taro (*Colocasia esculentum*)
Height/Spread: 60 in. × 48–60 in.
Hardy in zones 7–10

One of the realities of gardening with perennials is that it's difficult to get abundant floral display in heavy shade once spring is over. That's not to say, however, that shady beds need to be boring in summer—anything but, as this richly textured combination proves. Notice how important the large leaves of the taro and butterbur are.

1. White-variegated Japanese forest grass (*Hakonechloa macra* 'Alboaurea')
Height/Spread: 14 in. × 18–24 in.
Hardy in zones 5–8

2. Black mondo grass (*Ophiopogon planiscapus* 'Nigrescens')
Height/Spread: 9–12 in. × 9–12 in.
Hardy in zones 6–9

3. Feather-frond soft shield fern (*Polystichum setiferum* Plumoso-divisilobum Group)
Height/Spread: 24–36 in. × 36 in.
Hardy in zones 5–8

4. 'Krossa Regal' hosta (*Hosta* 'Krossa Regal')
Height/Spread: 30 in. × 36–60 in.
Hardy in zones 5–8

Nothing goes together like ferns and hostas unless it's ferns and grasses . . . or hostas and grasses. So why not mix all three? Here, you get not only a pleasing mixture of shapes, but also dramatic color contrast—blue, black, and gold. And the whole thing will look good for months on end.

1. Clary sage (*Salvia sclarea* var. *turkestanica*)
Height/Spread: 30–42 in. × 18–30 in.
Hardy in zones 5–10

2. 'Ostfriesland' meadow sage (*Salvia nemorosa* 'Ostfriesland')
Height/Spread: 18–30 in. × 18–24 in.
Hardy in zones 3–8

3. 'Cotswold Queen' mullein (*Verbascum* 'Cotswold Queen')
Height/Spread: 36–48 in. × 24 in.
Hardy in zones 5–9

Summertime, and the garden is tall. Especially when the sages and mulleins start to bloom. Clary sage is one of the most imposing, with enormous billows of pink (or white in the variety 'Album'). 'Ostfriesland' meadow sage is decidedly more dainty, but its deep blackish-purple is a good foil to the clary's sugar pink. Bright yellow 'Cotswold Queen' mullein keeps the mix lively.

1. Giant feather grass (*Stipa gigantea*)
Height/Spread: 96 in. × 48 in.
Hardy in zones 6–10

2. Hardy Jerusalem sage (*Phlomis russeliana*)
Height/Spread: 36 in. × 20 in.
Hardy in zones 4–10

3. White foxglove (*Digitalis purpurea* 'Alba')
Height/Spread: 48 in. × 24 in.
Hardy in zones 4–9 (biennial)

In case you've been cut off from civilization for the last couple of decades, ornamental grasses have become really big. And for good reason: they grow in shade; they grow in sun; there are short ones, tall ones, gold ones, blue ones . . . You get the idea. Giant feather grass is one of the biggies, shooting up to eight feet and more. Its tawny-gold flower heads positively glow when lit up by the sun.

1. 'Jupiter' ox-eye (*Heliopsis helianthoides* var. *scabra* 'Jupiter')
Height/Spread: 36–48 in. × 24–36 in.
Hardy in zones 3–9

2. 'Elmfreude' delphinium (*Delphinium* 'Elmfreude')
Height/Spread: 60 in. × 36 in.
Hardy in zones 3–8

3. 'His Majesty' goat's rue (*Galega ×hartlandii* 'His Majesty')
Height/Spread: 48–60 in. × 36 in.
Hardy in zones 3–9

Purple delphiniums and golden daisies—with a touch of lavender goat's rue: that's midsummer magic in the perennial garden. These plants all fall into the "big bruiser" category, so you need to give them plenty of space. And in the case of the delphinium, you'll need to do a fair amount of fertilizing and watering and maybe even—gulp—staking. Is it worth the trouble? You bet.

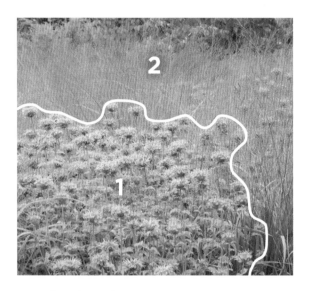

1. 'Pawnee' beebalm (*Monarda* 'Pawnee')
Height/Spread: 55–60 in. × 24–48 in.
Hardy in zones 3–9

2. 'Transparent' tall purple moor grass (*Molinia caerulea* subsp. *arundinacea* 'Transparent')
Height/Spread: 84 in. × 36 in.
Hardy in zones 4–9

Even though purple moor grass is not native to North America, this simple combination evokes the essence of the American prairie. With its densely clustered lilac flowers, 'Pawnee' beebalm is typical of the forbs (herbaceous flowering plants) that accompany prairie grasses.

1. 'Hidcote' English lavender (*Lavandula angustifolia* 'Hidcote')
Height/Spread: 12–24 in. × 12–18 in.
Hardy in zones 5–9

2. 'Silver Queen' white sage (*Artemisia ludoviciana* 'Silver Queen')
Height/Spread: 24 in. × 24 in. (spreading)
Hardy in zones 4–9

Want a little piece of Provence in your garden? Try this classic pairing of deep-purple 'Hidcote' lavender with intensely silvery white sage. While you won't need a mild, Mediterranean winter to succeed with these plants, you will need full sun and extremely well-drained soil.

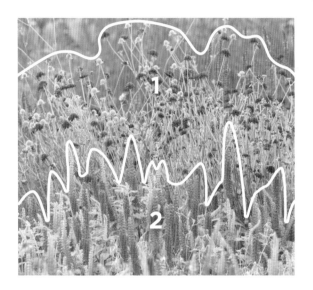

1. Crimson scabious (*Knautia macedonica*)

Height/Spread: 18–24 in. × 18–24 in.
Hardy in zones 5–9

2. Iranian germander (*Teucrium hircanicum*)

Height/Spread: 16–24 in. × 18 in.
Hardy in zones 5–9

As Thoreau said, "Simplify, simplify." It's good advice for the garden as well as for life. If creating a big impact is one of your goals, you'll be more likely to succeed (especially if your space is limited) with fewer rather than more plants. Focus on shape, don't go wild with color, and you'll be on the right track.

1. Hardy Jerusalem sage (*Phlomis russeliana*)
Height/Spread: 36 in. × 20 in.
Hardy in zones 4–10

2. 'Indigo' meadow sage (*Salvia pratensis* 'Indigo')
Height/Spread: 24–26 in. × 24–36 in.
Hardy in zones 3–8

When you're using complementary colors—like yellow and violet—bear in mind that they're more likely to marry well if they're not of equal intensity. If the violet is strong, pair it with a soft yellow, as here; if the yellow is strong, pair it with lavender or lilac. Or don't—sometimes breaking the rules brings wonderful surprises.

1. 'Kobold' blazing star (*Liatris spicata* 'Kobold')
Height/Spread: 18–30 in. × 18 in.
Hardy in zones 4–9

2. 'Chocolate' white snakeroot (*Eupatorium rugosum* 'Chocolate')
Height/Spread: 36–48 in. × 30 in.
Hardy in zones 4–9

3. 'Lucifer' crocosmia (*Crocosmia* 'Lucifer')
Height/Spread: 24–48 in. × 48 in.
Hardy in zones 5–9

Does the thought of placing magenta next to scarlet horrify you? Maybe you should reconsider—sometimes a slight shock can be good for the system. Especially when you include a "pacifier" like 'Chocolate' white snakeroot, colors that would ordinarily fight to the death suddenly become best friends.

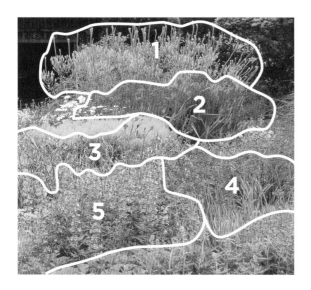

1. 'Lavandelturm' Culver's root (*Veronicastrum virginicum* 'Lavendelturm')
Height/Spread: 36–48 in. × 24–36 in.
Hardy in zones 3–8

2. 'Lucifer' crocosmia (*Crocosmia* 'Lucifer')
Height/Spread: 24–48 in. × 48 in.
Hardy in zones 5–9

3. 'Chicago Sunrise' daylily (*Hemerocallis* 'Chicago Sunrise')
Height/Spread: 28 in. × 18–24 in.
Hardy in zones 3–10

4. 'Isis' lily-of-the-Nile (*Agapanthus campanulatus* 'Isis')
Height/Spread: 30 in. × 24 in.
Hardy in zones 8–10

5. 'Stapleford Gem' beardtongue (*Penstemon* 'Stapleford Gem')
Height/Spread: 24 in. × 16 in.
Hardy in zones 7–9

This is what happens when you ignore all the rules about combining color and throw together a bunch of magnificent, late-summer-blooming plants: fabulousness! Monet might not like it, but Matisse sure would. Go ahead—be brave. Scarlet, yellow, mauve, violet, orange . . . someone get a camera! (Oh wait, someone did . . .)

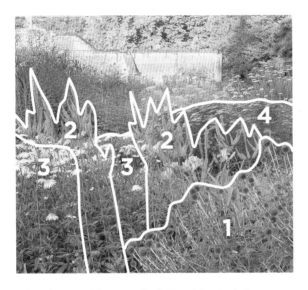

1. Globe thistle (*Echinops ritro*)
Height/Spread: 36–40 in. × 18–24 in.
Hardy in zones 3–8

2. 'Lavandelturm' Culver's root (*Veronicastrum virginicum* 'Lavendelturm')
Height/Spread: 36–48 in. × 24–36 in.
Hardy in zones 3–8

3. 'T. E. Killin' Shasta daisy (*Leucanthemum* ×*superbum* 'T. E. Killin')
Height/Spread: 30 in. × 24 in.
Hardy in zones 5–9

4. 'Summerwine' yarrow (*Achillea* 'Summerwine')
Height/Spread: 24 in. × 24–48 in.
Hardy in zones 3–8

There's something wonderfully whimsical about globe thistles—round balls of blueness on silvery white stems. (They're also a butterfly magnet.) There's no need for a referee when you're combining them with other flowers in lavender, white, and pink. In fact, this quartet might be a little too tame if it weren't for the diverting contrast of flower shapes.

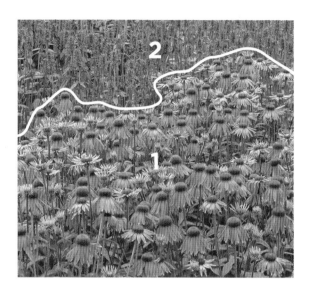

1. 'Kim's Knee High' purple cone-flower (*Echinacea purpurea* 'Kim's Knee High')
Height/Spread: 12–24 in. × 12–24 in.
Hardy in zones 3–8

2. 'Hummelo' betony (*Stachys officinalis* 'Hummelo')
Height/Spread: 18–24 in. × 18–24 in.
Hardy in zones 4–8

Call this inspired minimalism: just two plants in basically the same color range but with starkly contrasting shapes. Keep in mind that if you want to produce a sense of drama you're going to have to be lavish when you plant—say, at least a dozen each. A couple of measly little specimens isn't going to cut it.

1. 'Kobold' blanketflower (*Gaillardia* 'Kobold')
Height/Spread: 12 in. × 12 in.
Hardy in zones 3-9

2. 'Bluebird' delphinium (*Delphinium* 'Bluebird')
Height/Spread: 60-72 in. × 24 in.
Hardy in zones 3-8

3. 'Terracotta' yarrow (*Achillea* 'Terracotta')
Height/Spread: 36 in. × 30 in.
Hardy in zones 3-8

4. 'Picos Blue' sea holly (*Eryngium bourgatii* 'Picos Blue')
Height/Spread: 18 in. × 12 in.
Hardy in zones 5-9

5. 'Butterpat' sneezeweed (*Helenium* 'Butterpat')
Height/Spread: 48 in. × 24 in.
Hardy in zones 3-8

This combination recalls the happy, colorful confusion of a cottage garden. Yet there's method in the madness: the hot oranges and yellows of the blanketflower and yarrow are a canny match for the blue-violet delphinium and steel-blue sea holly. This is a fine example of making art seem artless (while having fun in the garden).

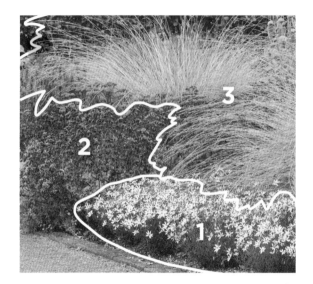

1. 'Moonbeam' threadleaf tickseed (*Coreopsis verticillata* 'Moonbeam')
Height/Spread: 18–24 in. × 24 in.
Hardy in zones 3–9

2. 'Rosenkuppel' ornamental oregano (*Origanum* 'Rosenkuppel')
Height/Spread: 18 in. × 18 in.
Hardy in zones 5–10

3. Atlas fescue (*Festuca mairei*)
Height/Spread: 12–36 in. × 20–36 in.
Hardy in zones 4–9

'Moonbeam' tickseed has become a star of the perennial garden, and deservedly so—for weeks in summer it covers itself with charming, pale-lemon daisies, and doesn't need to be fussed over. A perfect blender, it softens the reddish-purple of the 'Rosen-kuppel' oregano and brings out the gold undertones in the Atlas fescue.

1. 'Butterfly Blue' scabious (*Scabiosa* 'Butterfly Blue')

Height/Spread: 12–18 in. × 12–18 in.
Hardy in zones 5–9

2. Bowles' golden sedge (*Carex elata* 'Aurea')

Height/Spread: 18–30 in. × 18–30 in.
Hardy in zones 5–9

Pale lilac blue: such a nice, soothing color. You'd never dream of calling it boring, would you? Well, not if you pair it with the zingy chartreuse of Bowles' golden sedge. Because scabious has a prolonged blooming period, this combination will bring you weeks of pleasure.

1. 'Terracotta' yarrow (*Achillea* 'Terracotta')
Height/Spread: 36 in. × 30 in.
Hardy in zones 3-8

2. Hungarian bear's breeches (*Acanthus hungaricus*)
Height/Spread: 24-36 in. × 24-36 in.
Hardy in zones 5-9

3. Mexican feather grass (*Nassella tenuissima*)
Height/Spread: 24 in. × 12 in.
Hardy in zones 7-10

Contrasting shapes plus nuanced colors are guaranteed to produce a pleasing garden scene. Here, there is a lively interplay between the plate-shaped yarrow flowers, the wispy grass, and the boldly vertical bear's breeches. The russets and brownish purples constitute a winningly sophisticated palette.

1. 'Firebird' crocosmia (*Crocosmia ×crocosmiiflora* 'Firebird')
Height/Spread: 20–36 in. × 12–18 in.
Hardy in zones 6–9

2. 'Rosenkuppel' ornamental oregano (*Origanum* 'Rosenkuppel')
Height/Spread: 18 in. × 18 in.
Hardy in zones 5–10

3. 'Morning Light' maiden grass (*Miscanthus sinensis* 'Morning Light')
Height/Spread: 48–60 in. × 30–48 in.
Hardy in zones 5–9

With their outrageous colors, crocosmias could cause a traffic accident. But as long as you don't drive through your perennial border, you'll be fine. Just give them some good companions, like the rosy-flowered oregano and maiden grass shown here.

1. 'Black Adder' hyssop (*Agastache* 'Black Adder')
Height/Spread: 24–36 in. × 15 in.
Hardy in zones 6–9

2. 'Little Joe' coastal Joe-Pye weed (*Eupatorium dubium* 'Little Joe')
Height/Spread: 48 in. × 36 in.
Hardy in zones 4–9

If you want to attract butterflies to your garden, these two native North American plants will have them frantically fluttering in your direction. On top of that, they're handsome, long-blooming, tough perennials that will give your garden a sophisticated, "European New Wave" look.

1. 'Waltraut' sneezeweed (*Helenium* 'Waltraut')
Height/Spread: 36 in. × 24 in.
Hardy in zones 3-8

2. White narrow-leaf burnet (*Sanguisorba tenuifolia* 'Alba')
Height/Spread: 60 in. × 18-24 in.
Hardy in zones 4-9

The unfortunately named sneezeweeds (they are not known to aggravate allergies) come in a wide range of warm, earthy colors, which you can either accentuate or tone down. With its airy, graceful stems and dangling chenille-like flowers, white narrow-leaf burnet is a first-rate toner-downer. Just don't overdo it—you don't want the garden to turn into a snoozefest.

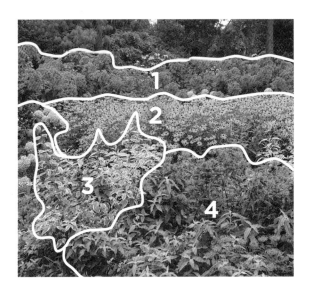

1. 'Gateway' Joe-Pye weed (*Eupatorium purpureum* subsp. *maculatum* 'Gateway')
Height/Spread: 48–60 in. × 24–36 in.
Hardy in zones 4–8

2. 'Goldsturm' black-eyed Susan (*Rudbeckia fulgida* var. *sullivantii* 'Goldsturm')
Height/Spread: 24–36 in. × 12–24 in.
Hardy in zones 3–9

3. 'White Gold' red-twigged dogwood (shrub) (*Cornus sericea* 'White Gold')
Height/Spread: 36–84 in. × 120 in.
Hardy in zones 3–8

4. 'Violet Queen' beebalm (*Monarda* 'Violet Queen')
Height/Spread: 36 in. × 24 in.
Hardy in zones 3–9

You probably wouldn't want to attempt this—mixing strong pinkish-purples with strong yellow—at any other time of year. But when the sun is strong, the temperature is high, and summer is at its peak, you can get away with it—especially if you mix in a bit of variegated foliage (like the dogwood's) to act as peace-maker.

1. Cardoon (*Cynara cardunculus*)
Height/Spread: 48–96 in. × 48 in.
Hardy in zones 7–10 (treat as annual in colder areas)

2. 'Sahin's Early Flowerer' sneeze-weed (*Helenium* 'Sahin's Early Flowerer')
Height/Spread: 36 in. × 18–24 in.
Hardy in zones 3–8

3. 'Prince Igor' red-hot poker (*Kniphofia* 'Prince Igor')
Height/Spread: 50 in. × 40 in.
Hardy in zones 7–10

If you have enough room, you should try growing a cardoon at least once in your gardening career (even if you live in an area colder than zone 7 and have to grow it as an annual). It's like having an enormous fountain of silver foliage erupting from the border—highly useful for toning down warmer colors. As a bonus, you also get purple-blue flowers like giant thistles (which is what a cardoon is, after all).

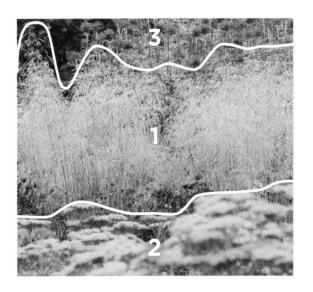

1. 'Goldtau' tufted hair grass (*Deschampsia cespitosa* 'Goldtau')
Height/Spread: 12–24 in. × 12–24 in.
Hardy in zones 4–8

2. 'Terracotta' yarrow (*Achillea* 'Terracotta')
Height/Spread: 14–24 in. × 14–18 in.
Hardy in zones 3–9

3. 'Scorpion' beebalm (*Monarda* 'Scorpion')
Height/Spread: 36 in. × 24 in.
Hardy in zones 3–9

A certain amount of fuzziness can be a good thing in the garden, particularly when it's supplied by blooming grasses in a handsome shade of gold. Grasses, in general, are excellent blenders and peace-keepers in the garden—as here, where 'Goldtau' tufted hair grass mediates between the orange yarrow and purple beebalm.

1. Leatherleaf sedge (*Carex buchananii*)
Height/Spread: 24 in. × 18 in.
Hardy in zones 7–10

2. 'Walker's Low' catmint (*Nepeta racemosa* 'Walker's Low')
Height/Spread: 30 in. × 36 in.
Hardy in zones 3–8

Copper is an intriguing color not often found in perennials, but leatherleaf sedge offers it in abundance. If using this somewhat unusual plant makes you nervous, pair it with something tried-and-true, like the catmint pictured here. The catmint's purple flowers are long-lasting, and its dense gray foliage makes an excellent foil for the sedge.

1. 'Brunette' bugbane (*Actaea simplex* 'Brunette')
Height/Spread: 60-70 in. × 24-28 in.
Hardy in zones 3-8

2. Himalayan cranesbill (*Geranium himalayense*)
Height/Spread: 12-18 in. × 24 in.
Hardy in zones 4-8

3. Variegated comfrey (*Symphytum ×uplandicum* 'Variegatum')
Height/Spread: 30 in. × 36 in.
Hardy in zones 5-8

4. 'Superba' bistort (*Persicaria bistorta* 'Superba')
Height/Spread: 24-30 in. × 24 in.
Hardy in zones 4-8

Sure, the flowers are lovely in this combination, but it's the foliage that steals the scene. The bugbane is a dramatic, deep chocolate brown; in late summer and early autumn it bears delicate, pinkish white bottle-brush flowers. Serving as a backdrop is variegated comfrey—one of the most striking shade-tolerant perennials in the gardener's repertoire.

1. White-striped creeping softgrass (*Holcus mollis* 'Albovariegatus')
Height/Spread: 4–8 in. × 12–24 in.
Hardy in zones 6–9

2. 'Emma' twinspur (*Diascia* 'Emma')
Height/Spread: 18 in. × 42 in.
Hardy in zones 8–10

Here we have two charming rompers, one demure (the grass), the other brazen (the twinspur). The creeping softgrass makes a handsome, moderately spreading groundcover—just be careful not to plant the plain green form, which can be highly invasive. The rambunctious twinspur is best treated as an annual in areas with cold winters.

1. Porcupine grass (*Miscanthus sinensis* 'Strictus')
Height/Spread: 70–80 in. × 36–60 in.
Hardy in zones 5–9

2. Pink mountain fleece (*Persicaria amplexicaulis* 'Rosea')
Height/Spread: 48 in. × 48 in.
Hardy in zones 5–8

Here's a fun game you can play: find a flower whose shape precisely mimics the shape of a companion foliage plant. In this case, the pairing will look good for many weeks, since mountain fleece is an exceptionally long-blooming perennial and the porcupine grass looks good from spring to autumn, and even beyond. Better still, it doesn't flop.

1. 'Scorpion' beebalm (*Monarda 'Scorpion'*)
Height/Spread: 36 in. × 24 in.
Hardy in zones 3–9

2. 'Rehbraun' panic grass (*Panicum virgatum 'Rehbraun'*)
Height/Spread: 48 in. × 18 in.
Hardy in zones 4–8

The interesting choice here is the switchgrass. Starting out a clear, light green, it gradually becomes more and more suffused with red, until by season's end you might almost mistake it for Japanese blood grass. Early on, however, it's a perfect match for the strong reddish purple of the beebalm.

1. Mop-headed sedge (*Carex flagellifera*)
Height/Spread: 10–16 in. × 16–24 in.
Hardy in zones 7–10

2. 'Karley Rose' Oriental fountain grass (*Pennisetum Orientale* 'Karley Rose')
Height/Spread: 48–60 in. × 36–48 in.
Hardy in zones 6–9

3. 'Cosmopolitan' maiden grass (*Miscanthus sinensis* 'Cosmopolitan')
Height/Spread: 84–108 in. × 36–48 in.
Hardy in zones 5–10

No doubt you're skeptical: nothing but grasses? It can work—but only if you're careful about choosing varieties with enough contrast. Here, there's contrast of both color and height—and the fountain grass has handsome pink flowers, to boot. What you *don't* want to do is to plant three varieties of copper-colored sedges together. Bor-ing!

This grouping is definitely not for the color-phobic. But if, like the poet William Blake, you believe that "exuberance is beauty," then this combination is about as beautiful as it gets. Interestingly, the main players are all members of the daisy family, and the similarity of habit and flower shape helps keep the exuberance from turning into a riot.

1. Sweet coneflower (*Rudbeckia subtomentosa*)
Height/Spread: 36–60 in. × 12–24 in.
Hardy in zones 4–9

2. 'Mrs. S. T. Wright' New England aster (*Aster novae-angliae* 'Mrs. S. T. Wright')
Height/Spread: 36 in. × 24 in.
Hardy in zones 4–8

3. 'Lye End Beauty' New England aster (*Aster novae-angliae* 'Lye End Beauty')
Height/Spread: 54 in. × 36 in.
Hardy in zones 4–8

4. 'Gullick's Variety' perennial sunflower (*Helianthus* 'Gullick's Variety')
Height/Spread: 60 in. × 36–48 in.
Hardy in zones 4–9

5. 'Gateway' Joe-Pye weed (*Eupatorium purpureum* subsp. *maculatum* 'Gateway')
Height/Spread: 48–60 in. × 24–36 in.
Hardy in zones 4–8

1. Lily-of-the-Nile (*Agapanthus campanulatus* subsp. *patens*)
Height/Spread: 24 in. x 12 in.
Hardy in zones 7-10

2. 'Crimson Beauty' sneezeweed (*Helenium* 'Crimson Beauty')
Height/Spread: 16-24 in. x 16 in.
Hardy in zones 3-8

Lilies-of-the-Nile are one of the great joys of late summer. (And they make great container plants if you live in a part of the country colder than zone 7.) Ranging from pure white to deepest blue-violet, they can sometimes appear a little cold unless paired with warmer colors. 'Crimson Beauty', one of the shorter-growing sneezeweeds, provides just the touch of heat needed to bring out the blue of the agapanthus.

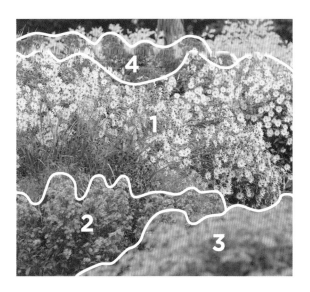

1. 'Lemon Queen' perennial sunflower (*Helianthus* 'Lemon Queen')
Height/Spread. 00 in. x 40 60 in.
Hardy in zones 4–9

2. 'Calliope' smooth aster (*Aster laevis* 'Calliope')
Height/Spread: 60–70 in. x 18–24 in.
Hardy in zones 4–9

3. 'Mönch' Frikart's aster (*Aster ×frikartii* 'Mönch')
Height/Spread: 24–36 in. x 12–18 in.
Hardy in zones 5–9

4. 'Glutball' Joe-Pye weed (*Eupatorium maculatum* 'Glutball')
Height/Spread: 72 in. x 48 in.
Hardy in zones 4–8

'Lemon Queen' is indeed a regal plant — large of stature and royally munificent with its gentle yellow flowers. Tolerant of both dry and wet soils, it's one of the most reliable and rewarding perennials you can grow. Pair it with a purple aster like 'Calliope', and you have almost instant garden gratification.

1. Rooper's red-hot poker (*Kniphofia rooperi*)
Height/Spread. 36 in. x 24 in.
Hardy in zones 7–10

2. 'Professor Anton Kippenberg' New York aster (*Aster novi-belgii* 'Professor Anton Kippenberg')
Height/Spread: 14–20 in. x 18 in.
Hardy in zones 4–9

3. 'Snowbank' false aster (*Boltonia asteroides* var. *latisquama* 'Snowbank')
Height/Spread: 36–48 in. x 36–48 in.
Hardy in zones 4–9

There's nothing subtle about red-hot pokers, but that's the key to their appeal—you get a big, shaggy wad of bright color on the end of a long, narrow stem. In late summer, when the garden is bursting with daisies of various sorts, they can be just the thing for keeping the border lively.

1. 'Karneol' sneezeweed (*Helenium* 'Karneol')
Height/Spread: 36 in. × 24 in.
Hardy in zones 3-8

2. 'Silver Comet' pampas grass (*Cortaderia selloana* 'Silver Comet')
Height/Spread: 48-60 in. × 48-60 in.
Hardy in zones 8-10

3. Pink mountain fleece (*Persicaria amplexicaulis* 'Rosea')
Height/Spread: 48 in. × 48 in.
Hardy in zones 5-8

In combining perennials, particularly for summer display, it doesn't do to be too fastidious about color—your carefully planned harmonies are as likely to misfire as not. Pay more attention to shape: the flow of grasses next to the buttons of sneezeweed in front of the spires of mountain fleece—you'll be guaranteed an interesting garden picture. (Although 'Silver Comet' pampas grass is not known to produce unwanted seedlings, California gardeners may want to steer clear of it.)

1. 'Spark's Variety' monkshood (*Aconitum* 'Spark's Variety')
Height/Spread: 24–48 in. × 18–24 in.
Hardy in zones 3–8

2. 'Incomparibilis' ox-eye (*Heliopsis helianthoides* var. *scabra* 'Incomparibilis')
Height/Spread: 36–48 in. × 24–36 in.
Hardy in zones 4–9

The moody, mysterious monkshoods are always fascinating (not to mention highly poisonous—handle with care!), but they need cheerful company; moody is one thing, clinically depressed is quite another. Yellow daisies, like the fluffy double 'Incomparibilis' ox-eye, are the cockeyed optimists of the flower world, always ready to brighten the corners where they are.

1. 'Rozanne' cranesbill (*Geranium* 'Rozanne')

Height/Spread: 18–20 in. × 18–24 in.
Hardy in zones 5–8

2. 'Matrona' stonecrop (*Sedum telephium* 'Matrona')

Height/Spread: 24–30 in. × 18–24 in.
Hardy in zones 3–9

3. 'Loraine Sunshine' ox-eye (*Heliopsis* 'Loraine Sunshine')

Height/Spread: 30 in. × 16 in.
Hardy in zones 4–9

We all love flowers, but amid the floral crescendo of late summer, it's worthwhile to pay attention to foliage. Here the outstanding examples are dusky 'Matrona' stonecrop and variegated 'Loraine Sunshine' ox-eye. Of course, an ocean of blue-violet 'Rozanne' cranesbill lapping at their feet doesn't hurt things.

1. 'Calliope' smooth aster (*Aster laevis* 'Calliope')
Height/Spread: 60-70 in. × 18-24 in.
Hardy in zones 4-9

2. 'Lye End Beauty' New England aster (*Aster novae-angliae* 'Lye End Beauty')
Height/Spread: 54 in. × 36 in.
Hardy in zones 4-8

3. 'Lemon Queen' perennial sunflower (*Helianthus* 'Lemon Queen')
Height/Spread: 80 in. × 48-60 in.
Hardy in zones 4-9

4. Variegated maiden grass (*Miscanthus sinensis* 'Variegatus')
Height/Spread: 60-84 in. × 48-60 in.
Hardy in zones 5-9

5. 'Chieftain' blue wood aster (*Aster cordifolius* 'Chieftain')
Height/Spread: 24-48 in. × 18-24 in.
Hardy in zones 3-8

This combination is almost *too* pretty. Those big mounds of pink, purple, and lavender asters are the floral equivalent of cotton candy. Thank goodness someone had the presence of mind to plant the yellow sunflower. Otherwise your gums might start to recede.

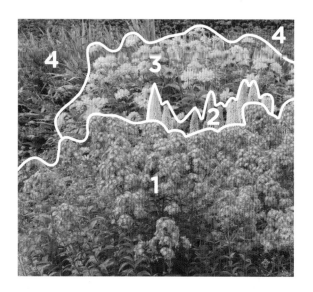

1. 'Branklyn' garden phlox (*Phlox paniculata* 'Branklyn')
Height/Spread: 36 in. x 24 in.
Hardy in zones 3–8

2. 'Percy's Pride' red-hot poker (*Kniphofia* 'Percy's Pride')
Height/Spread: 36 in. x 24 in.
Hardy in zones 6–10

3. 'Bressingham Doubloon' ox-eye (*Heliopsis* 'Bressingham Doubloon')
Height/Spread: 48–60 in. x 24–36 in.
Hardy in zones 3–9

4. 'Emberglow' crocosmia (*Crocosmia* 'Emberglow')
Height/Spread: 24–36 in. x 12 in.
Hardy in zones 5–9

The great German nurseryman Karl Foerster once said, "Life without phlox is an error." You might be inclined to agree once you've bloomed them in your garden and reveled in their color and fragrance. Their mound-shaped flower heads benefit from contrasting shapes—like the red-hot pokers and ox-eyes used here.

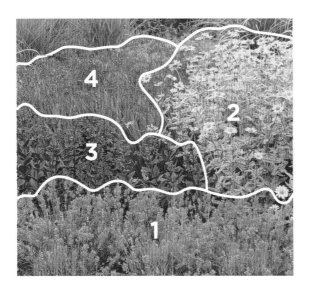

1. 'Blue Cushion' English lavender (*Lavandula angustifolia* 'Blue Cushion')
Height/Spread: 16 in. × 16 in.
Hardy in zones 5–8

2. 'Loraine Sunshine' ox-eye (*Heliopsis* 'Loraine Sunshine')
Height/Spread: 30 in. × 16 in.
Hardy in zones 4–9

3. 'Matrona' stonecrop (*Sedum telephium* 'Matrona')
Height/Spread: 24–30 in. × 18–24 in.
Hardy in zones 3–9

4. 'Bressingham Blaze' crocosmia (*Crocosmia* 'Bressingham Blaze')
Height/Spread: 24–36 in. × 24 in.
Hardy in zones 5–9

If you took pure, undiluted oil paint right from the tube and brushed it fearlessly across a very large canvas, you might get a picture like this. You could call it "The Joy of Color." Notice that the dark-leaved stonecrop actually makes the other colors seem brighter—a useful trick to have up your sleeve.

1. 'Othello' garden phlox (*Phlox paniculata* 'Othello')
Height/Spread. 30 in. × 24 in.
Hardy in zones 3–8

2. 'Waltraut' sneezeweed (*Helenium* 'Waltraut')
Height/Spread: 36 in. × 24 in.
Hardy in zones 3–8

3. White narrow-leaf burnet (*Sanguisorba tenuifolia* 'Alba')
Height/Spread: 60 in. × 18–24 in.
Hardy in zones 4–9

Have you ever seen those funny/stupid videos that come with the warning, "Don't try this at home"? Well, *do* try this one at home, even if your inner color consultant shudders at the idea of putting a deep magenta phlox next to a yellow-and-orange sneezeweed. Gardening isn't for sissies.

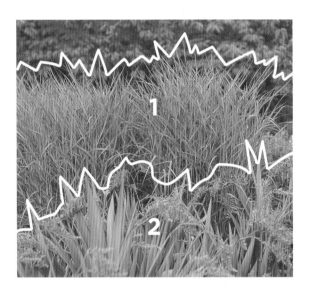

1. 'Heavy Metal' panic grass (*Panicum virgatum* 'Heavy Metal')
Height/Spread: 48–60 in. x 16–24 in.
Hardy in zones 5–9

2. 'Firebird' crocosmia (*Crocosmia ×crocosmiiflora* 'Firebird')
Height/Spread: 20–36 in. x 12–18 in.
Hardy in zones 6–9

Remember when you used to drive your parents nuts by playing your Iron Maiden albums with the stereo volume turned all the way up? Well, now you can pay tribute to those heady days of youth by planting 'Heavy Metal' panic grass. While it's not exactly metallic—more of a nice greenish blue—it *is* very pretty, and looks great with the orange 'Firebird' crocosmia. It's kind of like Judas Priest meets Igor Stravinsky.

1. 'Rubinzwerg' sneezeweed (*Helenium* 'Rubinzwerg')
Height/Spread: 24–30 in. × 15 in.
Hardy in zones 3–8

2. 'Black Adder' hyssop (*Agastache* 'Black Adder')
Height/Spread: 24–36 in. × 15 in.
Hardy in zones 6–9

3. 'Magnus' purple coneflower (*Echinacea purpurea 'Magnus'*)
Height/Spread: 24–60 in. × 18 in.
Hardy in zones 3–9

There's no point in trying to be too subtle in late summer—pastels look washed out in the strong light. Go for saturated hues—the purple of the hyssop, the orange-red of the sneezeweed, the strong rose of the coneflower—and let them clash away merrily. Do, however, pay attention to form, which, if carefully orchestrated, will take away the curse from even the most violent color contrasts.

172

1. 'Matrona' stonecrop (*Sedum telephium* 'Matrona')
Height/Spread: 24-30 in. × 18-24 in.
Hardy in zones 3-9

2. 'Canary Bird' crocosmia (*Crocosmia ×crocosmiiflora* 'Canary Bird')
Height/Spread: 30 in. × 12-16 in.
Hardy in zones 5-9

3. 'Patricia' cranesbill (*Geranium 'Patricia'*)
Height/Spread: 12-18 in. × 18-24 in.
Hardy in zones 5-9

4. Variegated maiden grass (*Miscanthus sinensis* 'Variegatus')
Height/Spread: 84 in. × 36-48 in.
Hardy in zones 5-10

Here's another lesson in toning things down. Now, it's perfectly all right to put a magenta cranesbill next to a bright yellow crocosmia, but you may want to add a muted, purplish stonecrop and a nice variegated grass to show the world you haven't utterly taken leave of your senses.

1. 'Blue Spire' Russian sage (*Perovskia* 'Blue Spire')
Height/Spread: 24–480 in. × 24–36 in.
Hardy in zones 5–9

2. 'Hadspen Abundance' Japanese anemone (*Anemone hupehensis* 'Hadspen Abundance')
Height/Spread: 36 in. × 24 in.
Hardy in zones 5–8

3. 'Firetail' mountain fleece (*Persicaria amplexicaulis* 'Firetail')
Height/Spread: 48 in. × 48 in.
Hardy in zones 5–8

4. 'Andenken an Alma Pötschke' New England aster (*Aster novae-angliae* 'Andenken an Alma Pötschke')
Height/Spread: 66 in. × 48–60 in.
hardy in zones 4–8

5. 'Karl Foerster' feather reed grass (*Calamagrostis* ×*acutiflora* 'Karl Foerster')
Height/Spread: 72 in. × 18 in.
Hardy in zones 4–8

Smoldering reds and purples are just what you want as summer eases into autumn. OK, you can throw in some pink Japanese anemones too. After all, they go nicely with the aster and mountain fleece, and they're superb with the Russian sage (which, by the way, is one of the most rewarding and long-blooming perennials you can grow).

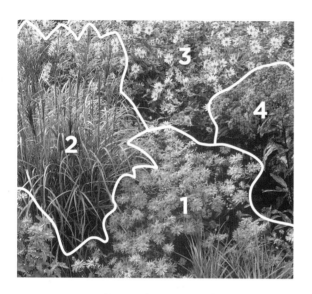

1. 'Mönch' Frikart's aster (*Aster ×frikartii* 'Mönch')
Height/Spread: 24–36 in. × 12–18 in.
Hardy in zones 5–9

2. 'Rotsilber' maiden grass (*Miscanthus sinensis* 'Rotsilber')
Height/Spread: 48–60 in. × 36 in.
Hardy in zones 5–9

3. Five-nerve helianthella (*Helianthella quinquenervis*)
Height/Spread: 48–72 in. × 36–48 in.
Hardy in zones 4–9

4. 'Glutball' Joe-Pye weed (*Eupatorium maculatum* 'Glutball'
Height/Spread: 72 in. × 48 in.
Hardy in zones 4–8

Daisies (or any plant with daisylike flowers) and grasses seem made for each other—maybe it's because they occur together so often in nature. When you bring them together in the garden, you evoke a powerful image of nature's harmony and unstudied beauty. It doesn't hurt, of course, that Frikart's aster is one of the longest-blooming perennials around, providing lavender-blue flowers for months.

1. Japanese blood grass (*Imperata cylindrica* 'Red Baron')
Height/Spread: 12–24 in. × 24–36 in.
Hardy in zones 6–9

2. Mexican feather grass (*Nassella tenuissima*)
Height/Spread: 24 in. × 12 in.
Hardy in zones 7–10

Now, it takes a fair amount of guts to restrict yourself to just two plants in an area this big. And it takes even more guts to use grasses rather than plants with more conspicuous flowers. But the result is a wonderful celebration of texture, and it has the advantage of looking good for months rather than weeks or days.

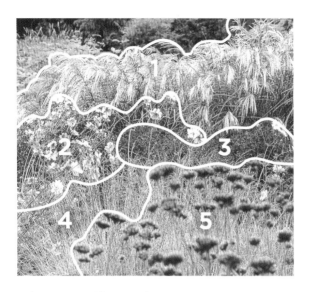

1. 'Kaskade' maiden grass (*Miscanthus sinensis* 'Kaskade')
Height/Spread: 60–84 in. × 36–60 in.
Hardy in zones 5–10

2. 'Königin Charlotte' Japanese anemone (*Anemone* ×*hybrida* 'Königin Charlotte')
Height/Spread: 24–36 in. × 24 in.
Hardy in zones 5–8

3. 'Freda Ballard' New York aster (*Aster novi-belgii* 'Freda Ballard')
Height/Spread: 36 in. × 24 in.
Hardy in zones 4–8

4. Striped purple moor grass (*Molinia caerulea* subsp. arundinacea 'Variegata')
Height/Spread: 84 in. × 36 in.
Hardy in zones 4–9

5. Tall verbena (*Verbena bonariensis*)
Height/Spread: 24–48 in. × 18–36 in.
Hardy in zones 7–10 (treat as annual in colder areas)

When grasses bloom and start to take on a tawny coloring, you know that summer is winding down. But autumn brings a whole new season to enjoy in the garden, with delights like Japanese anemone, tall verbena, and stonecrop. With the onset of cooler weather, deep, rich hues come to the fore.

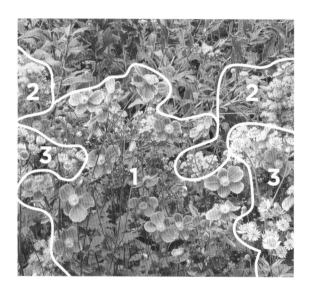

1. 'Abundance' Japanese anemone (*Anemone hupehensis* 'Hadspen Abundance')
Height/Spread: 36 in. × 24 in.
Hardy in zones 5–8

2. Upright goldenrod (*Solidago rigida*)
Height/Spread: 36–60 in. × 18–30 in.
Hardy in zones 3–9

3. Pink masterwort (*Astrantia major* var. *rosea*)
Height/Spread: 24 in. × 12 in.
Hardy in zones 6–9

Goldenrod has gotten a bad rap. "Weedy," some people say; "common" say others. But upright goldenrod is a perfectly respectable citizen of the perennial garden. Here, it echoes the yellow center of the Japanese anemone and lends warmth to the rather neutral buff-pink of the masterwort.

1. Hungarian daisy (*Leucanthemella scrotina*)
Height/Spread: 36–72 in. × 24–36 in.
Hardy in zones 4–9

2. 'Lemon Queen' perennial sunflower (*Helianthus* 'Lemon Queen')
Height/Spread: 80 in. × 48–60 in.
Hardy in zones 4–9

Certain floral combinations inevitably recall classic food pairings. If your favorite meal is breakfast, then these two daisies might make you think of fried eggs, but if you're a dessert fan, they're more like a nice big slice of lemon meringue pie. Now, isn't that a pleasant thought to have in the garden? Unless, of course, it makes you hungry.

1. 'Lady Gilmour' Japanese anemone (*Anemone* ×*hybrida* 'Lady Gilmour')

Height/Spread: 60 in. × 30 in.
Hardy in zones 5–9

2. Bowles' golden sedge (*Carex elata* 'Aurea')

Height/Spread: 18–30 in. × 18–30 in.
Hardy in zones 5–9

If you're a true color freak (in other words, if you spend more than ten minutes a day coordinating your clothes and accessories), you can have endless hours of fun in the garden. Here, for example, there's an exact match between the yellow and green center of the Japanese anemone and the foliage of the sedge. Goosebumps!

1. Wallich's spurge (*Euphorbia wallichii*)
Height/Spread: 24 36 in. × 24 in.
Hardy in zones 6–9

2. 'Jungfrau' Frikart's aster (*Aster ×frikartii* 'Jungfrau')
Height/Spread: 18–24 in. × 12–18 in.
Hardy in zones 5–9

3. 'Jennine' crocosmia (*Crocosmia* 'Jennine')
Height/Spread: 288 in. × 24 in.
Hardy in zones 6–9

When we think of the glories of autumn foliage, it's usually a blazing maple or aspen that comes to mind. Perennials, however, can also make a contribution, long after their flowers have faded. In fact, if your garden is small, it makes sense to use as many of these two-season plants as possible. With its exceptionally long blooming season, Frikart's aster can also claim to span the seasons.

1. 'Herbstfreude' ('Autumn Joy') stonecrop (*Sedum* 'Herbstfreude')

Height/Spread: 18–24 in. x 18–24 in.
Hardy in zones 3–9

2. 'Karl Foerster' purple moor grass (*Molinia caerulea* subsp. *arundinacea* 'Karl Foerster')

Height/Spread: 84 in. x 36 in.
Hardy in zones 4–9

As a friend of mine used to say, your feelings about autumn joy stonecrop may be influenced by your feelings about broccoli. Guess what? They're both good for you. Autumn is when the stonecrop comes into its glory, deepening into tones of richest crimson, and making a noble companion for golden ornamental grasses.

1. 'Pritchard's Giant' bugbane (*Actaea simplex* 'Pritchard's Giant')

Height/Spread: 70 in. × 24–28
Hardy in zones 3–8

2. Smooth violet prairie aster (*Aster turbinellus*)

Height/Spread: 48 in. × 24 in.
Hardy in zones 3–8

No, "bugbane" doesn't sound very pleasant, but these stately perennials are true winners, with bold, divided leaves and delicate wands of white flowers. The late-blooming varieties, like 'Pritchard's Giant', can easily steal the scene in the autumn garden, while beckoning seductively to asters and other lovelies.

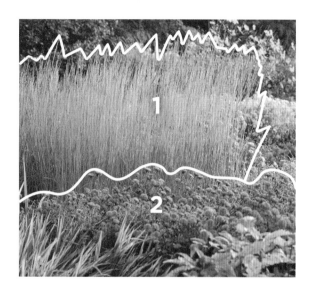

1. 'Karl Foerster' feather reed grass (*Calamagrostis* ×*acutiflora* 'Karl Foerster')
Height/Spread: 72 in. × 18 in.
Hardy in zones 4–8

2. 'Coombe Rosemary' New York aster (*Aster novi-belgii* 'Coombe Rosemary')
Height/Spread: 32 in. × 24 in.
Hardy in zones 3–8

In case you thought gardening was all stuffy and serious, this combination should convince you otherwise. How could you not smile after seeing the purple pompoms of 'Coombe Rosemary' New York aster? Of course, a visual joke can get boring if pushed too far. That's why the dignified, upright 'Karl Foerster' feather reed grass works so well here—it keeps the hilarity in check.

1. 'Ferner Osten' maiden grass (*Miscanthus sinensis* 'Ferner Osten')
Height/Spread: 10–60 in. × 36–48 in.
Hardy in zones 5–9

2. 'Loch Hope' lily-of-the-Nile (*Agapanthus* 'Loch Hope')
Height/Spread: 48 in. × 28 in.
Hardy in zones 8–10

3. Cutleaf staghorn sumac (tree) (*Rhus typhina* 'Dissecta')
Height/Spread: 15–25 ft. × 15–25 ft.
Hardy in zones 4–8

Silver and gold—that's what you get when maiden grass flowers reach their magnificent maturity, when lily-of-the-Nile ripens its fruits, and when staghorn sumac (actually a tree, but you can keep it compact through merciless pruning) turns to flame. Earlier in the summer, 'Loch Hope' lily-of the-Nile bears gorgeous, deep indigo flowers.

1. Feathertop (*Pennisetum villosum*)
Height/Spread: 24–30 in. × 30–36 in.
Hardy in zones 8–10

2. Japanese blood grass (*Imperata cylindrica* 'Red Baron')
Height/Spread: 12–24 in. × 24–36 in.
Hardy in zones 6–9

The fussy white flowers of the charmingly named feathertop would be great for a tickle fight, but maybe that's not something you're in the habit of doing in the garden. If you just want to look at them, you might as well pair them with Japanese blood grass, which reaches the peak of its rich coloration in the autumn.

1. 'Juli' maiden grass (*Miscanthus sinensis* 'Juli')
Height/Spread: 48 in. × 36 in.
Hardy in zones 5–9

2. 'Glutball' Joe-Pye weed (*Eupatorium maculatum* 'Glutball')
Height/Spread: 72 in. × 48 in.
Hardy in zones 4–8

German bred perennials ('Juli' means July and 'Glutball' means glowing ball) are often top-notch, even if their names don't exactly roll easily off of English-speaking tongues. Many retain their attractiveness well into autumn, as long as you cultivate an appreciation of the many rich variations of brown, ochre, and gold.

1. Roscoea (*Roscoea humeana*)
Height/Spread: 8–12 in. × 6 in.
Hardy in zones 7–9

2. Striped Japanese iris (*Iris ensata* 'Variegata')
Height/Spread: 20 in. × 20 in.
Hardy in zones 5–9

If you were to see these plants in summer, decked with rosy purple (the roscoea) and blue-violet (the iris) flowers, you'd never guess that they'd reach a second peak of beauty many months later, thanks to their narrow, tapering leaves. The ability to arrange this kind of agreeable surprise is the sign of a skilled—or very lucky—gardener.

1. 'Bressingham Ruby' heartleaf bergenia (*Bergenia* 'Bressingham Ruby')
Height/Spread: 14 in. × 12 in.
Hardy in zones 3–10

2. Mexican feather grass (*Nassella tenuissima*)
Height/Spread: 24 in. × 12 in.
Hardy in zones 7–10

In early spring, bergenias bear clusters of flowers in white, pink, or deep rose, but it's only with the onset of cold weather that their foliage begins to reveal its beauty, turning a deep cordovan or burgundy (at least in varieties like 'Bressingham Ruby'). The super-fine dried blades of Mexican feather grass deftly emphasize the textured, leathery bergenia leaves.

1. 'Kim's Knee High' purple coneflower (*Echinacea purpurea* 'Kim's Knee High')
Height/Spread: 12–24 in. × 12–24 in.
Hardy in zones 3–8

2. Tall verbena (*Verbena bonariensis*)
Height/Spread: 24–48 in. × 18–36 in.
Hardy in zones 7–10 (treat as annual in colder areas)

Yes, perennials die down in the winter; that doesn't mean that they disappear. Resist the urge to cut down the spent stalks of your summer-blooming perennials and you'll be rewarded with scenes of pure magic when hoarfrost decorates the sere seed heads. The birds will thank you, too (in their way), for leaving them a winter meal.

USDA WINTER HARDINESS ZONES

AVERAGE ANNUAL MINIMUM TEMPERATURE

Temperature (deg. C)	Zone	Temperature (deg. F)
Below −45.5	**1**	Below −50
−42.8 to −45.5	**2a**	−45 to −50
−40.0 to −42.7	**2b**	−40 to −45
−37.3 to −40.0	**3a**	−35 to −40
−34.5 to −37.2	**3b**	−30 to −35
−31.7 to −34.4	**4a**	−25 to −30
−28.9 to −31.6	**4b**	−20 to −25
−26.2 to −28.8	**5a**	−15 to −20
−23.4 to −26.1	**5b**	−10 to −15
−20.6 to −23.3	**6a**	−5 to −10
−17.8 to −20.5	**6b**	0 to −5
−15.0 to −17.7	**7a**	5 to 0
−12.3 to −15.0	**7b**	10 to 5
−9.5 to −12.2	**8a**	15 to 10
−6.7 to −9.4	**8b**	20 to 15
−3.9 to −6.6	**9a**	25 to 20
−1.2 to −3.8	**9b**	30 to 25
1.6 to −1.1	**10a**	35 to 30
4.4 to 1.7	**10b**	40 to 35
Above 4.4	**11**	Above 40

INDEX